March of America Facsimile Series

Number 101

Bibliography for March of America Series

Albert T. Klyberg

A Critical Bibliography
for The March of America Series

Albert T. Klyberg

ANN ARBOR

UNIVERSITY MICROFILMS, INC.

A Subsidiary of Xerox Corporation

Bibliography for March of America Series

Introduction

The discovery of a new and unsuspected continent, inhabited by people of an unimagined color and a primitive culture, was a shock to the western world such as we in America shall not experience. Our current "moon shots" are not comparable. In 1492 it was truly a "New World" that burst upon the European consciousness.

After the initial astonishment, exploration became an almost endless and beckoning adventure. Vespucci, Cabot, Magellan, Cartier, and Drake traced the coast lines. Once the two great continents were outlined, what lay in the interior? Cortes, De Soto, Champlain, Coronado, Smith, Marquette, La Salle and others told us. The filling of these continents was an experience running on four centuries after Columbus and accomplished by numerous and less known figures that we lump together under the term *pioneers*.

The March of America is in one sense a finished story, a closed chapter in our history. But because it lasted so many generations, embraced so many problems, and was repetitive in certain aspects, the experience undoubtedly shaped American outlook and American character. The westward movement was an achievement, a testing, a tragedy at times, and a triumph. It gave us values, vices, goals, virtues; it provided us with accumulated experience in government, law, private and public enterprise, education, transportation, church expansion, utilization of natural resources, and assimilation of newer immigrants. It bred in us mobility, restlessness, a willingness to experiment. In brief, it made us distinctive from the older nations of Europe.

Such a broad and significant effort as filling a continent is one we can never repeat ourselves; nor did our ancestors enjoy more than a segment of it in their own generation. From today's vantage point, however, we can leaf back through the printed word and learn how it was to see with the eyes of discovery, to settle in the wilderness with a pioneer, to build a community with neighbors. From the rich literature of *Americana* a hundred books of narration and description have been selected to make that past come alive. The books gradually focus on accomplishment in the United States, where history's meaning is most valid for us. They begin with Columbus' report of his first voyage, published in 1493; and they end with the essay by Professor Frederick Jackson Turner in 1893 on the closing of the last frontier.

Every book considered for inclusion in this Series was weighed for its authenticity. How well did the writer know of what he wrote? Was he a participant, an eye-witness, or a contemporary with access to the participants and their reports? Was the book influential? Was the author biased or prejudiced? The purpose was to assemble primary or source materials on which modern historians draw for the summaries found in textbooks. The Series was designed to be a source of stimulation to high school students and a research tool for college students. Both groups may go behind the scene provided by modern textbook authors, meet directly the men who ventured to the New World and on across the continent, and catch the flavor of their first-hand reports.

Certain other factors influenced the choice of books. Geographical balance was essential, and so the opening of every region is represented —not every state, but all regions. In a few areas and periods, such as the California Gold Rush, many titles were available, and selectivity is high. In the first two centuries, while several European powers were exploring America, English translations of foreign language books were chosen, since this Series was not meant to involve an exercise in translation merely for the sake of reproducing a first edition. Nevertheless, two source books are offered in foreign tongues, one in French and one in Spanish, to appeal to those readers with language skills and to remind others of the need for such skills even for the study of an area that is predominantly English speaking.

There is a time balance as well as a geographical distribution. The Series covers four centuries, four hundred years of the westward march of America. In the first century, 1493 to 1593, there are fifteen books. The second century, 1593 to 1693, shows eighteen titles; as does the next century, 1693-1793. The final period, 1793-1893, is illuminated by forty-nine books. Some concession was made to the availability of hardback modern reprints of old books in that they were weighed against similar and equally useful books that have not been reprinted. We believe this Series can stand alone in its coverage of the westward course of civilization across America.

After the successive periods of exploration, almost all the books are by persons who migrated in order to settle, as distinguished from accounts by promoters and foreign visitors. The list is by no means exclusively social history, filled with commentaries on the customs of various regions. Neither is it military history, for books about wars and campaigns have been omitted. Wars interrupted or turned the westward march, but did not stop it. Indian hostilities, on the other hand, were the price of expansion and they are not neglected. Primarily the Series is descriptive of ever unfolding regions, of the dangers and satisfactions of pushing back the wilderness, of the task of expanding a nation.

Now that the frontier is closed, the continent fulfilled, the qualities that were needed for this labor of four centuries may no longer be requisite to maintaining the amalgamated society we have evolved. Whatever readjustments may be necessary, they must be worked out in full and vivid comprehension of exactly the challenges met during four hundred years of effort throughout America.

Most of the original books from which these offset facsimiles were made are extremely scarce and expensive. They are not to be seen in public or college libraries. They are preserved in special collections like the University of Michigan's William L. Clements Library, where this project took shape. Further, the facsimiles are not offered in forbidding isolation; each book has a foreword, all of which were written at The Folger Shakespeare Library in Washington, D.C. under the coeditorship of Dr. Louis B. Wright, Director, and Dr. Philip A. Knachel, Assistant Director. The writing of these forewords, which highlight the significance of each book was done by members of the Folger staff: Elaine W. Fowler, Philip A. Knachel, Nati Krivatsy, Virginia LaMar, Megan Lloyd, Joan Morrison, Lilly Stone, and Louis B. Wright. The critical bibliography following this introduction was prepared by Albert T. Klyberg, MA, doctoral candidate in American history and research assistant at the Clements Library. In addition, a set of catalogue cards from the Library of Congress accompanies the Series.

Howard H. Peckham, Director.

William L. Clements Library
University of Michigan
Ann Arbor, Michigan
June 1966

Acknowledgments

As in any such endeavor there are many individuals who contribute ideas and energy without whose assistance little would have been accomplished. The original impetus for a comprehensive reprint series of Americana was provided by Mr. Eugene B. Power and Mr. Stevens Rice of University Microfilms Inc., and the resulting series took shape under the supervision of Howard H. Peckham, Director of the William L. Clements Library. The full facilities of the Library were made available to the compiler, notably the very fine bibliographical section. Endless technical queries and bibliographic problems were solved with the patient help of Mrs. Georgia C. Haugh, Rare Book Librarian. Mr. Donald L. Poroda of the University of Michigan Undergraduate Library, Prof. Jean Hecht of Columbia University, Mr. Nathaniel N. Shipton, Map and Print Librarian at Clements Library, and Professors Helen K. Osgood and Ernest S. Osgood of the College of Wooster likewise contributed suggestions and aid. The Rare Book Room of the University's General Library was cooperative in lending books for the project, as was the John Carter Brown Library, The Henry E. Huntington Library, The Library of Congress, and the British Museum.

A.T.K.

A briefe and true report
of the new found land of Virginia,
of the commodities and of the nature and man=
ners of the naturall inhabitants. Difcouered by
the Englifh Colony there feated by Sir Richard
Greinuile Knight In the yeere 1585. Which Rema
=ined Vnder the gouernement of twelue monethes,
At the fpeciall charge and direction of the Honou=
rable SIR WALTER RALEIGH Knight lord Warden
of the ftanneries Who therein hath beene fauoured
and authorifed by her MAIESTIE
and her letters patents:
This fore booke Is made in Englifh
By Thomas Hariot feruant to the abouenamed
Sir WALTER, a member of the Colony, and there
imployed in difcouering ·

CVM GRATIA ET PRIVILEGIO CÆS.MA.TIS SPECIA.:

FRANCOFORTI AD MOENVM
TYPIS IOANNIS WECHELI, SVMTIBVS VERO THEODORI
DE BRY ANNO CIↃ IↃ XC.
VENALES REPERIVNTVR IN OFFICINA SIGISMVNDI FEIRABENDII

TITLE PAGE.
(reduced 30%)
From March Of America Series No. 15

Bibliography

All of the books reprinted in the March of America Series are in the collection of the William L. Clements Library of American History at the University of Michigan in Ann Arbor, unless otherwise noted. Since all of the books are old, some pages are stained or otherwise disfigured. Of course such imperfections show in the printed copies to some extent, although every care was taken to minimize these objections wherever possible.

The number of the book in the collection is followed by the name of the author, the title, the publisher, and place and date of publication.

1. **Colombo, Cristoforo.** *Epistola de insulis nuper inventis.* [Rome, Plannck, after 29 April 1493.] and *The Columbus letter of 1493...* a new translation into English by Frank E. Robbins. Ann Arbor, The Clements Library Associates, 1952.

   Columbus' report to Ferdinand and Isabella in 1493 was the first published account of land beyond the ocean sea by someone who had been there. It is the fundamental starting place for a study of the history of America. As far as we know, no account of prior discovery by Indians, Norse, Welsh, or shipwrecked mariners exists.

   Quickly translated into Latin—the universal language of scholars—and first published in Rome, the report was printed in large editions through the use of the newly-devised printing press, and was widely circulated. Seventeen editions were published and it was translated into several languages before 1500. It awoke the western world and turned Europe's attention from the Mediterranean to the Atlantic.

2. **Waldseemüller, Martin.** *Cosmographiae introductio cum quibusdam geometriae ac astrono miae principiis ad eam rem necessariis. Insuper quattuor Americi Vespucii navigationes...* [St. Die, Lud, 1507]

and *The cosmographiae introductio of Martin Waldseemüller...* translation and introduction by Joseph Fischer and Franz von Wieser, edited by Charles George Herbermann. New York, U.S. Catholic Historical Society, 1907.

The New World was named "America" in 1507 when Martin Waldseemüller, a German geographer and teacher, suggested this name as a fitting tribute to the mainland explorations of Amerigo Vespucci. The suggestion appeared in an introduction to world geography which accompanied two world maps published in 1507 by Waldseemüller. Four letters or reports of Vespucci's reputed voyages also appeared with this work.

While geographers in northern Europe adopted the suggestion, geographers in the Iberian peninsula, where Vespucci was held to be merely a member of several exploring parties, continued to refer to the New World as the "Indies."

This copy of the *Cosmographiae Introductio* (St. Die, September, 1507) is accompanied by an English translation from the 1907 facsimile published by the United States Catholic Historical Society, reproduced here by permission of the Society. This translation, made by Professors Joseph Fischer, S. J., and Franz von Wieser and edited by Dr. Charles George Herbermann, was actually made for a different edition. However, the only difference in the editions was the format of the preliminary dedicatory pages. The first thirty pages and the translators' introduction have been omitted. The folding diagram from the facsimile has been substituted for the original, which was imperfect.

3. Münster, Sebastian. *A treatyse of the newe India...* translated out of Latin into Englishe. By Rycharde Eden. [London, Sutton, 1553.]

One of the first books in English to relate the voyages of Columbus and Vespucci was Sebastian Münster's *Treatyse of the Newe India*. It was translated into English by Richard Eden in 1553. Eden was a forerunner of Richard Hakluyt, the most famous compiler of exploration narratives.

Münster's account of the early voyages was taken from his *Cosmographiae Universalis*, a world geography published in

Basel, in 1544. The Eden translation is very rare. The copy used for this series is from the British Museum, London. Only the second section, which concerns America, has been reproduced.

4. **Anghiera, Pietro Martire d'.** *The Decades of the newe worlde or west India...by Peter Martyr of Angleria and translated into Englysshe* [from Latin] *by Rycharde Eden.* In Eden, Richarde, ed. *The decades of the newe worlde or west India...*London, 1555.

The first historian of America was Peter Martyr, or Pietro Martire Anghiera. He knew Columbus, Vespucci, and many of their contemporaries. The first English translation of Martyr's *Decades* was completed by Richard Eden in 1555. Like his translation of Sebastian Münster in 1553, it was one of the first books on America in English.

The selections in the work reproduced here are: Decades I-IV, the "Bull of Alexander VI," "The Summary History of Fernandez Oviedo," and "Magellan's Voyage around the World." Oviedo was the first Spanish chronicler of the new world. Eden himself made a significant contribution by noting in his preface the voyage of the Cabots in 1497, upon which rested Britain's claims in North America. Decade IV begins on leaf 149 but the original printer continued to carry "The Thyrde Decade" on the running heads.

5. **[Hakluyt, Richard.]** comp. *Divers voyages touching the discoverie of America, and the ilands adjacent unto the same...*London, Woodcocke, 1582.

This book by Hakluyt, perhaps the greatest writer of navigation narratives, is the first in English to refer to any part of what is now the United States.

Among the interesting items in the book is a translation into English of the "letters patentes" granted by Henry VII to John Cabot, on whose voyages of discovery England's claims in North America were later based.

Voyages of Cabot, Giovanni da Verazano, and Jean Ribaut, the French adventurer who led the first Huguenot expedition to Florida, are also chronicled.

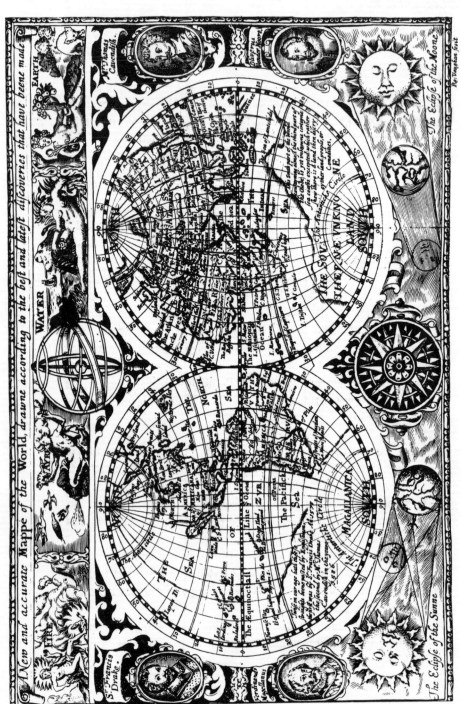

MAP OF THE WORLD.
(reduced 23%)
From March Of America Series No. 11

6. [Gómara, Francisco López de.] *The pleasant historie of the conquest of the Weast India, now called new Spayne*...translated out of the Spanish tongue by T. N., London, Bynneman [1578].

In 1519 Hernando Cortes began his conquest of Mexico. It marked the first large-scale clash between medieval European and native American civilizations. Francisco López de Gómara, the author of this account, was the private secretary of Cortes, and wrote from Cortes' letters and documents many years later in Spain.

De Gómara's work first appeared in English under the translated title in 1578. This London edition was the second portion of the Spanish editions of 1552 and 1553. However, the prejudice in favor of Cortes is maintained.

7. Díaz del Castillo, Bernal. *The true history of the conquest of Mexico...written in the year 1568*...translated from the original Spanish, by Maurice Keatinge. London, Wright, 1800.

In contrast to the official account by López de Gómara of Cortes' conquest of Mexico, Bernal Díaz del Castillo presents the point of view of the common soldier in the expedition. A weathered veteran of the old world's wars, Díaz recounts the savagery of the new world and the wonderment of the ancient Aztec civilization.

Díaz's account, written in 1568, was first translated into English in 1800 by Maurice Keating in London.

8. Casas, Bartolomé de las. *The Spanish Colonie, or Briefe Chronicle of the Acts and gestes of the Spaniardes in the West Indies, called the newe Worlde*...translated into english, by M. M. S. London, Broome, 1583.

In 1552 Bartolomé de las Casas, a Spanish priest and friend of the king, printed a series of tracts in Seville which assailed the treatment of the Indians by the Spaniards. His vivid descriptions of massacres and harsh cruelty were seized upon by Spain's rivals, France and England, and spread far and wide as hostile propaganda. This was the origin of the so-called "black legend" of Spanish misrule of America.

The earliest English edition of this book was printed in London in 1583. The first in a long line of American reformers, Las Casas' efforts had questionable results: the new laws he obtained were disobeyed, and slaves from Africa began to replace Indian labor.

9. **Nuñez Cabeza de Vaca, Alvar.** *Relation of Alvar Nuñez Cabeça de Vaca*, translated from the Spanish by Buckingham Smith. New York, [Munsell] 1871.

The first account of travels in what is now the United States was written by Alvar Nuñez Cabeza de Vaca, a member of the Spanish expedition which landed in Florida in 1528. What followed was an amazing tale of adventure, mishap, and wandering for nine years until he reached the Rio Grande and settlements in northern Mexico. Cabeza de Vaca's narrative popularized the notion of the fabled seven cities of Cibola, where great wealth was reputedly stored.

The account was first published in 1542; the first English translation was made in 1851. The Buckingham Smith translation, now republished, was first published in 1871.

10. **[Cartier, Jacques.]** *A Shorte and briefe narration of the two navigations and discoveries to the northweast partes called Newe Fraunce: first translated out of French into Italian by...Gio: Bapt: Ramutius, and now turned into English by John Florio...*London, Bynneman, 1580.

Jacques Cartier was one of the many navigators who searched for a northwest water passage through America to the riches of the orient. Discovering the Gulf of the Saint Lawrence in 1534, he believed he had found the fabled passage to the Pacific. In a subsequent voyage the next year he realized his error. What he had found was one of the great waterways to the interior of North America. It was the key route which made the development of the great fur empire possible.

John Florio, the translator of this account of Cartier's two voyages, was a friend of William Shakespeare. It is the first book in English on New France.

11. [Drake, Sir Francis, 1st bart.] comp. *The world encompassed by Sir Francis Drake, being his next voyage to that to Nombre de Dios formerly imprinted...*London, Bourne, 1628.

The exploits and adventures of Sir Francis Drake were represented as sort of a one-man war against the transmarine commerce of the Spanish empire, and loom very large in the accounts of the English challenge to Spanish preeminence in the New World. Swooping down on Spanish treasure ships with impunity, he enriched the royal coffers of England while enlivening the spirits of his countrymen with the tales of his daring.

One of the important aspects of his 1577 voyage, however, was not his outwitting of the Spanish but his careful exploration of the Gulf of California and his landing near the site of modern San Francisco. He named the territory New Albion, and his claim was cited during the 19th century controversy over control of the Pacific Northwest.

The account of this famous voyage, *The World Encompassed* ...was taken from the notes of the chaplain, Francis Fletcher who may have conducted the first Anglican service in California. Drake's nephew, bearing the same name as the famous navigator, was the compiler of this work.

12. Hakluyt, Richard, tr. *Virginia richly valued, by the description of the maine land of Florida...Written by a Portugall gentleman of Elvas...*London, Kyngston, 1609.

The quest for gold, fabled cities, and mysterious fountains of youth caused many Spanish adventurers to wander through the southern and southwestern areas of what is now the United States. Hernando de Soto led such a trek in 1539. It lasted four years and covered the present states of Florida, Georgia, the Carolinas, Tennessee, Alabama, Mississippi, Arkansas, Oklahoma, and Texas. De Soto himself lost his life at the Mississippi River.

An account of this expedition was published in Portugal in 1557. The first edition in English, *Virginia Richly Valued*, was published by Richard Hakluyt in 1609.

13. Winship, George Parker, ed. *The journey of Coronado, 1540-1542 ...as told by himself and his followers.* New York, Allerton, 1922.

The tale told by Cabeza de Vaca of fabulous cities of gold fired the imagination of his countrymen in Spain. In 1540 an expedition under Francisco Vazquez de Coronado set out from the west coast of Mexico and traveled through what is now the southwest United States in quest of the cities. Instead of wealth they discovered and were awed by such natural wonders of the region as the Grand Canyon.

Coronado's march was recorded by Pedro Castañeda. George Parker Winship translated the Spanish manuscript of Castañeda into English in 1896, and it was published separately as *The Journey of Coronado* in 1922.

14. **Hakluyt, Richard.** *The Relation of David Ingram* from *The principall navigations, voyages and discoveries of the English nation...* London, Bishop and Newberie, 1589.

The history of the frontier and westward movement is a story crowded with huge portions of myth and many varieties of tall tales. For better or worse, men were influenced by what they hoped, and were often swayed by purely promotional rhetoric.

One of the most intriguing tales of the late sixteenth century is the story of David Ingram and two companions who supposedly walked across the continent west to east from Rio Panuco in Mexico to a river near Cap Breton Island in Canada.

Richard Hakluyt printed the story in his 1589 edition of his *Principall Navigations*, but becoming skeptical about its veracity he omitted it from his later editions. Modern scholars are undecided about its truthfulness. However, it made a great impression on contemporary Englishmen, including those luckless settlers who were lured by such stories to Raleigh's newly founded colony at Roanoke.

Only the Ingram story has been reproduced from Hakluyt's *Principall Navigations*, under the title, *The Relation of David Ingram.*

15. **Bry, Theodore de, ed.** *A briefe and true report of the new found land of Virginia...In the yeere 1585...At the speciall charge and direction of...Sir Walter Raleigh...This fore booke is made in English by Thomas Hariot.* Frankfort am Main, Wecheli, 1590.

The first account of the first English colony in America was written by one of the colonists, Thomas Hariot. The colony was attempted on Roanoke Island, off the coast of North Carolina, in 1585 under the auspices of Sir Walter Raleigh. The colonizers were unsuccessful and returned to England the next year. Hariot was undismayed and wrote this descriptive account of the "new found land" with its trees and plants, the animals and the Indians, and the great prospects for future settlement. It was published at London in 1588.

Theodore de Bry, a publisher and engraver in Frankfurt, Germany, asked to reprint it in four languages to sell throughout Europe. He also found some watercolors painted at Roanoke by John White, another colonist, and added a sketch of the original savage inhabitants of England, the Picts. De Bry engraved the illustrations for his edition of 1590. His English language version is reproduced here from the copy in the William L. Clements Library, which also owns the 1588 first edition.

16. Brereton, John. *A briefe and true relation of the discoverie of the north part of Virginia...Made this present yeere 1602...*London, Bishop, 1602.

The Pilgrims were the first white settlers in New England, but prior to their coming in 1620, fishermen and navigators had explored this area, then called "Northern Virginia."

The first description of New England was made by John Brereton in 1602. In this account he tells of the activities of the party under Captains Gosnold and Gilbert. The group landed at Cuttyhunk Island at the entrance to Buzzard's Bay. A fort was erected, but the settlement was temporary.

17. Rosier, James. *A true relation of the most prosperous voyage made this present yeere 1605...*London, Bishop, 1605.

One of the members of the 1602 expedition to New England was James Rosier. Three years later in 1605 he returned to the area with Captain George Weymouth. They landed on the coast of Maine, exploring Monhegan Island and the Kennebec River.

Brereton's, *A briefe and true relation of the discoverie of the*

north part of Virginia (1602) and Rosier's account comprise
what is known as "The Verie Two Eyes of New-England, Historie."

18. **Smith, John.** *The Generall Historie of Virginia, New-England, and
the Summer isles...from...1584 to this present 1624.* London, I.D.
and I.H., 1624.

Of all the pamphlets and books about Virginia which were written by Captain John Smith, the 1624 edition of *The Generall
Historie of Virginia* was probably the most important, the most
elaborate in illustration, and the most difficult for rare book collectors to obtain.

Combining many of his previous accounts of Virginia and
helping himself to the writings of others, he set about to rectify
the injustice done him by the Virginia Company, which ousted
him after he succeeded in establishing a permanent colony. His
account of his deliverance by Pocohantas in 1608 is part of the
material which is genuinely new and genuinely Smith's.

According to Philip L. Barbour's excellent work, *The Three
Worlds of Captain John Smith* (Boston, 1964), Smith was in such
a hurry to get his defense into print that he utilized two printers,
each doing a separate section. This accounts for the pagination
gap; the first printer ran out of material in signature N. (A signature is a printed sheet which is folded and cut to form a section
of pages in a book.) Smith submitted some verses to fill out the
incomplete signature, and signature O was left out completely.
The second printer had been instructed to begin signature P on
page 105.

19. **Purchas, Samuel.** *Henry Hudson's Voyages* from *Purchas his Pil-
grimes*...London, Stansby, 1625. Part 3.

The quest for a northern passage to the East dominated Henry
Hudson's career as a navigator and explorer, and he undertook
four voyages to find it. The first two, in 1607 and 1608 under
the Muscovy Company of England, were directly north and then
east along the northern coast of Russia. On both of these he was
thwarted by ice. His third voyage, sponsored by the Dutch East
India Company in 1609, sent him west in search of a northwest

passage. The result was discovery of the Hudson River, and led to the founding of the New Netherland colony. Hudson's fourth voyage was far to the north; he discovered and explored the large bay in northern Canada which now bears his name, and where he and a few loyal companions were abandoned to their death in an open boat.

The accounts of Hudson's voyages were published by Samuel Purchas, the literary heir of the great chronicler Hakluyt. Only Part III, the portion relating the voyages of Hudson, is reproduced here.

20. Champlain, Samuel de. *Les voyages du sieur de Champlain Xaintongeois...*Paris, Berjon, 1613.

Samuel de Champlain, navigator, explorer, geographer, trader, founder, and administrator, was from 1603 until 1635 the dominant figure in the area of North America which came to be known as New France.

Having explored and mapped the coast from Nova Scotia to Maine, and even as far south as Cape Cod, in his first two voyages, Champlain set about establishing a post at Quebec on his third voyage in 1608. Sending young men to make contact with the Indians, he won the loyalty of the tribes opposed to the Iroquois Confederacy. His travels inland led him as far south as the lake which we know now as Lake Champlain.

His second work, *Les Voyages* (Paris, 1613), covers the events from 1603 to 1613, and provides the first account of the first permanent French settlement in the New World. This richly illustrated work is in French.

21. Mourt's relation. *A relation or Journall of the beginning and proceedings of the English plantation setled at Plimoth in New England...*London, Bellamie, 1622.

The earliest account of the first permanent settlement in New England is this journal of the first year at Plymouth, September 1620 to December 11, 1621. Probably written by William Bradford and Edward Winslow, it is a primary source for stories of the exploits of Captain Myles Standish and the Pilgrims' relations with the Indians.

THE TOWNE OF POMEIOOC.
(reduced 40%)
From March Of America Series No. 15

This is often called Mourt's Relation because the preface was signed by a George Mourt. The copy used for this series is from the Library of Congress.

22. *A relation of Maryland; together, with a map of the countrey, the conditions of plantation, His Majesties Charter to the Lord Baltemore,* translated into English. London, Peasley, 1635.

Cecil Calvert, second Lord Baltimore, was a first-rate businessman. In 1635 he directed the preparation of a book entitled *A Relation of Maryland*...Printed in London the same year, it was neither the first nor the last promotional tract enticing Englishmen to come to America, but it was one of the best.

The famous narrative of Father Andrew White describing the beginnings of Maryland was condensed and used for the first part. Then followed a complete description of the country, Indian policy, conditions for land tenure, and detailed instructions to the planters. The accompanying map is of interest because of the boundary disputes which later arose between Virginia and Maryland.

23. Mason, John. *A brief history of the Pequot War: especially of the memorable taking of their fort at Mistick in Connecticut in 1637.* Boston, Kneeland and Green, 1736.

The friendly relations with the Indians which the Pilgrims enjoyed became strained as more and more white men came to New England. Finally in 1637 war broke out between the settlers and the Indians as the first wave of immigrants moved into the new lands of the Connecticut Valley. This first inland frontier beyond the beaches produced the first armed resistance in the North, the Pequot War.

Of the four accounts of this war, the best is by Major John Mason, the commander of the Connecticut forces. It was published almost 100 years later in 1736 in Boston.

24. Bland, Edward. *The discovery of New Brittaine. Began August 27. Anno Dom. 1650. by Edward Bland, Abraham Woode, Sackford Brewster, Elias Pennant...*London, Harper, 1651.

Less than fifty years after the first English settlement at Jamestown, settlers were moving up-country from the tidewater to the piedmont. In 1650, one of the first parties to reconnoiter the Virginia frontier was that of Edward Bland, Captain Abraham Wood, and two others who went south to Carolina. Bland called the country "New Brittaine."

The original pamphlet in the William L. Clements Library is the only one in this country to contain the accompanying map.

25. Lederer, John. *The discoveries of John Lederer, in three several marches from Virginia to the west of Carolina...Collected and translated out of Latine from his discourse and writings, by Sir William Talbot.* London, J. C., 1672.

John Lederer was a German physician who made three expeditions between 1669 and 1670 to the Blue Ridge Mountains. Like the party of Bland and Wood, he was one of the vanguard of Virginians who sought a way through the western mountains to the rivers which led to the southern sea about which the Indians spoke.

Although Lederer tended to embroider his accounts with marvels, and his remarks about a reputed trip to Carolina are probably fabricated, he was the first white man on record to look over the mountains into the valley of Virginia.

26. Denton, Daniel. *A brief description of New-York: formerly called New-Netherlands.* London, Hancock, 1670.

Denton's *New York* is the earliest known description of the hub of the middle colonies. Appearing in 1670, just six years after the British took over New York from the Dutch, this work is a fine example of promotional literature. Like all literature of this type it confronts the reader with the vexing problem of separating the accurate information about the climate and land conditions from the exaggerations and distortions which are intended to lure newcomers.

Denton describes the physical characteristics of the New York area and gives an agricultural inventory of the natural and cultivated crops, as well as a list of the game. Particularly interesting is his informative and succinct account of Indian life and customs.

27. Danckaerts, Jasper. *Journal of a voyage to New York, and a tour in several of the American colonies in 1679-80, by Jaspar Dankers and Peter Sluyter.* Translated...and edited by Henry C. Murphy. Brooklyn [Long Island Historical Society], 1867.

Life in the Middle Colonies in the late 17th century had few more perceptive observers than Jaspar Danckaerts who was a member of the Labadist sect, a small group in the Calvinist tradition. His purpose in traveling through the Middle Colonies in the year 1679-1680 was to locate a place where these Protestant reformers could set up a community for their faith. He was successful in making arrangements for such a site in Maryland.

His journal, however, is more than just an account of an emissary seeking out the "promised land"; it is a rich account of Dutch New York and the residue of Dutch influence in the Delaware Valley. His trips to Maryland, to Albany, and later to New England are filled with remarks about the people, institutions, and life of what was then still the frontier. The manuscript was discovered in Holland and first translated into English by Henry C. Murphy of the Long Island Historical Society in 1867.

28. Marquette, Jacques. "Voyages du P. Jacques Marquette, 1673-75," in *The Jesuit relations and allied documents: Travels and explorations of the Jesuit missionaries in New France, 1610-1791,* edited by Reuben Gold Thwaites. Cleveland, Burrows Bros., 1896-1901. v. 59.

The British Colonists had been probing the Appalachian barrier for passes to the interior since 1650, but it was the French in 1673 who gained the great valley of the Mississippi and posed a man-made barrier to further British penetration with a string of forts and posts which eventually stretched from Niagara to New Orleans.

The first representatives of the French empire to explore the Mississippi were the intrepid Jesuit Father Jacques Marquette, and Louis Jolliet. The account of their amazing expedition through Indian country and down the Mississippi comes to us from Marquette's journal in two parts. The first part concerns the trip down the Mississippi from the Illinois River to the Arkansas, the second Marquette's subsequent trip to the Illinois country.

The journal is but a small piece of the great body of exploration literature written by the Jesuits. Between the years 1632 and 1673 annual reports were sent by the Superior of the Canadian Mission to the Provincial of the Order at Paris. These reports were published and became known as *The Jesuit Relations*. Publication of these reports was halted in 1672; thus Marquette's Journal, though certainly a worthy account, is not one of the *Jesuit Relations*. When Reuben Gold Thwaites edited the *Jesuit Relations, and Allied Documents, 1610-1791* he included Marquette's Journal as one of the allied documents. It is from this edition that we have reproduced the present copy. The original French text and the accompanying English translation appear on facing pages.

29. *King Philip's War Narratives: The present state of New-England, with respect to the Indian war. London, 1675. A continuation of the state of New-England; being a farther account of the Indian warr. London, 1676. A new and further narrative of the state of New-England being a continued account of the bloody Indian War. London, 1676. A true account of the most considerable occurrences that have hapned in the warre between the English and the Indians in New-England. London, 1676. The war in New-England visibly ended. London, 1677.*

In 1675, almost forty years after the Pequot War in the Connecticut Valley, Indian resentment against the encroachment of the New England town system once again flared into violent hostility. Under the leadership of King Philip, the Wampanoags, the Narragansetts, the Mohegans, the Podunks, and the Nipmucks spread devastation and destruction. In the course of the war twelve towns were destroyed, and half the towns in New England were damaged. Ultimately the Indians' will to fight was broken when their fields and villages were systematically reduced to ashes.

Among the numerous books and pamphlets which the New

Englanders produced to record the war was a group of five folio tracts in the nature of war bulletins. They appeared at intervals between 1675 and 1677. Only a few pages in length, they were written by various people in Boston and sent to London to be published. As long ago as the 1880's they were regarded as "among the choicest rarities of a New England library."

30. Hennepin, Louis. *A description of Louisiana. Translated...* by John Gilmary Shea. New York, Shea, 1880.

Following the lead of Marquette and Jolliet, Robert Cavalier, Sieur de La Salle and his assistants Tonti, Hennepin, and Joutel furthered the development of the Mississippi Valley empire. La Salle was quick to see the possibilities for trade and continental supremacy for France.

Frustrated by rival economic interests, national and international religious rivalries, national, colonial and imperial party politics, greed, petty jealousy, and the raw vagaries of the frontier wilderness itself, he lost his fortune, his friends, and ultimately his life. Though he failed personally, through his efforts posts were established, trade contacts were cemented, and the great territory of Louisiana became French in fact as well as in name.

One of the accounts by an associate of La Salle was Father Louis Hennepin's *A Description of Louisiana* (1683). Hennepin accompanied La Salle from Fort Frontenac on Lake Ontario to Niagara. There the "Griffon," the first ship on the Great Lakes, was constructed. They sailed to Green Bay and on its return voyage the "Griffon," loaded with fur, was lost. Hennepin continued with La Salle to the Illinois country, where they parted. Hennepin traced the Illinois River south to its confluence with the Mississippi, then turned north and explored the Mississippi to the Falls of St. Anthony.

Although Hennepin's later editions have been largely discredited, his first is regarded as a bonafide account. Hennepin's importance derives from his position as one of the first truly popular writers about French America. Hennepin's first work was translated into English in 1880 by John Gilmary Shea. It is the Shea translation which we have reprinted for this Series.

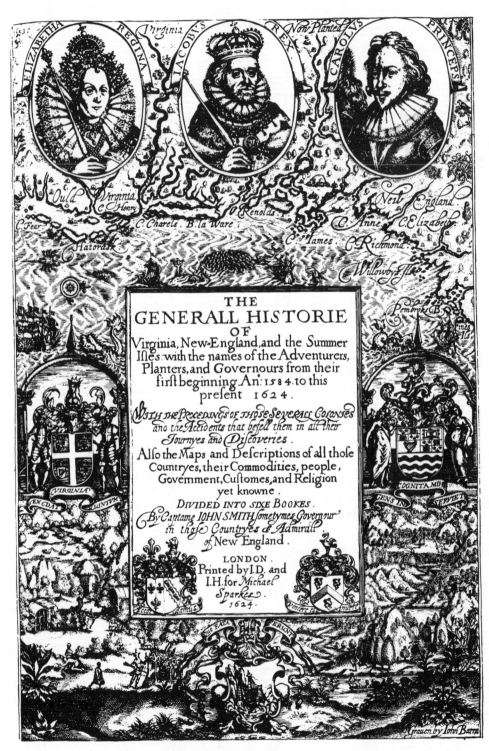

TITLE PAGE.
(reduced 28%)
From March Of America Series No. 18

31. Joutel, Henri. *A journal of the last voyage perform'd by Monsr. de La Sale, to the Gulph of Mexico*...London, Bell, 1714.

The account of La Salle's attempts to establish a French post at the mouth of the Mississippi comes to us by way of Henri Joutel, a member of the company of La Salle's 1685 voyage. La Salle missed the mouth of the Mississippi and the party wandered in vain along the Texas coast. Although Joutel was not implicated in the conspiracy against La Salle, he tacitly took part by keeping La Salle's death from being made public. Despite this defect in his character, his account is one of the best.

The original manuscript was mutilated on several occasions before it was finally published. The abridged form appeared in Paris in 1713. The following year a translation of this version was published in London. Thus far the full manuscript has not been published in English.

32. Budd, Thomas. *Good order established in Pennsilvania & New-Jersey in America*...[n.p.] 1685.

In 1685 a printer by the name of William Bradford came to Philadelphia and set up a press. One of the first products of the press was Thomas Budd's *Good Order* (1685). Another example of promotional literature, it catalogues the fruits, grains, and vegetables of the Delaware Valley as well as noting the possibilities for trade with the West Indies, the establishing of schools, banks and industries.

Thomas Budd came to West Jersey in 1678 and served on the governor's council. A man of property and considerable influence, he maintained a keen interest in the development of the Delaware Valley until his death in 1698. A copy of this rare early work is in the Clements Library; the copy used for this Series was obtained from The Library of Congress.

33. Fallows, Arthur. *Journal* from "Discoveries beyond the Appalachian Mountains in September, 1671" by David I. Bushnell, Jr. in "American Anthropologist" n.s., IX (1907).

The efforts to penetrate the frontier-mountain barrier in the South were led by Governor Berkeley of Virginia and Captain Abraham Wood. It was Berkeley who sent John Lederer on three expeditions, recorded in *The Discoveries of John Lederer.* Wood, who ran Ft. Henry at the falls of the Appomattox, sent out two parties in 1671 and 1673.

The first, led by Thomas Batts and Arthur Fallows (or Robert Fallam), went west along the Staunton River through the Blue Ridge until they reached the westward flowing New River, a tributary of the Ohio. The second group, under James Needham and Gabriel Arthur, ventured south, where they met the Savannah and Tennessee Rivers. In the next twenty years others followed these two blazed trails that pointed the way to the streams feeding into the Mississippi.

The expedition of Batts and Fallows was recorded in Arthur Fallow's *Journal.* Note that the author is variously referred to as Arthur Fallows or Robert Fallam. Two copies of this journal were made: one by Dr. Daniel Coxe and one by the Reverend John Clayton. The Coxe copy is in the British Public Record Colonial Papers and was published in the New York Colonial Documents (1853).

The Clayton Copy was sent and read to the Royal Society. It was first published by David Bushnell, Jr. in the "American Anthropologist." The Clayton Copy as published by Bushnell has been selected for reprinting in this Series because it appears to be more complete than the Coxe copy.

34. Williams, John. *The redeemed captive returning to Zion...*6th ed. Boston, Hall, 1795.

As the French continued to strengthen their grip on the great continental interior of America in the late 17th century, and as the English settlers moved up the valleys of the Atlantic coast pressing back the Indians and threatening the fur empire of the French, it was natural that there would be conflicting claims and challenges by rival empires.

From 1689 to 1763 there were four colonial wars in America between England and France. To be sure, although the wars were a part of the global struggle for supremacy they were more than this. At issue was the control of North America, a competition between two distinct colonial systems, and the question of religious diversity versus orthodoxy.

John Williams was a Puritan minister in Deerfield, Massachusetts during King William's and Queen Anne's Wars (1689-1713). When Deerfield was attacked in 1704, he and his family were taken captive by the Indians and imprisoned in Canada. His account of their captivity is a classic; some twenty editions have occurred since the first in 1707. The sixth edition of 1795 was selected because it contains additional materials in the appendix which throw light on some of the wider aspects of the war.

35. Lawson, John. *A new voyage to Carolina...* London, 1709.

Because of wrangles among the proprietors and civil strife which characterized periods of 17th century settlements in Virginia and Maryland, there was a steady migration south to the colony of Carolina.

Eight proprietors were granted Carolina in 1663. Within ten years there were two centers of development: Charlestown, and the Albemarle Sound area.

By 1700 when John Lawson, a young Englishman, arrived, the colony's foothold in the Southern wilderness was secure. Lawson traveled through this wilderness, taking note of the land, its products, potential, and the inhabitants. His account is one of the more perceptive, witty, and better written early frontier reports. Lawson became Surveyor-General of North Carolina, and while engaged in surveying a few years after his book appeared, he was seized by Tuscarora Indians and burned to death.

36. Charlevoix, Pierre François Xavier de. *Journal of a voyage to North-America...* London, Dodsley, 1761. 2 v.

In 1761 a two-volume edition of Father Pierre Charlevoix's *Journal* appeared in English. This first English edition was a translation of volume three of his larger work, *History and General Description of New France,* which was published in French in 1744. The *Journal* begins with a historical discourse on the origin of the American Indian, and is followed by thirty-six letters addressed to the Duchesse de Lesdiguierres, 1720-1723. These letters give an account of Charlevoix's travels through the Great Lakes area and down the Mississippi.

While Charlevoix did not contribute new discoveries, his work is the best written account by the early explorers. As a result, he was widely read, particularly for his descriptions of Indians, who were a great source of curiosity for 18th century Europeans.

37. Stephens, William. *A journal of the proceedings in Georgia, beginning October 20, 1737* ...London, Meadows, 1742. v. 1 & 2.

The territory which we now know as Georgia was originally part of the Carolina proprietorship. Failing to develop any settlements in this southernmost region, the proprietors surrendered their claims to the Crown. In 1732 a new group led by James Oglethorpe was granted the land. Oglethorpe wished to establish a social experiment where debtors and unemployables could start a new life. As well as providing a new chance for the poor, the colony would be a buffer, protecting the southern flank of the colonies from the encroachments of the Spanish and the raids of the Indians.

The most detailed account of the affairs or events of the province are in the diary of William Stephens. Stephens at one time was secretary to the colony's trustees and later became President of the colony. The *Journal* is very rare, and a complete set of three volumes is difficult to find. Volumes one and two have been reprinted for this Series.

38. Venegas, Miguel. *A natural and civil history of California*...London, Rivington and Fletcher, 1759. 2 v.

Almost up until the beginning of the 18th century, Spanish knowledge about the country north of Mexico, called California, was fairly limited; indeed for a long time the southern California peninsula was considered to be a large island. The increasing appearances of British ships and, later, the presence of Russian traders in Alaska, inspired the Spaniards to push their boundaries northward up the coast. Initially this task fell to the Jesuits, who were anxious to expand their missionary activity. Men like Fathers Kino and Salvatierra led the way; the soldiers and traders followed.

The first work in English to record the activities of these pioneer efforts and to describe the characteristics of the country was Miguel Venegas' *Civil History of California* (London, 1759). The work is actually an abridgment of Father Andrés Marcos Burriel's *Noticia de la California* (Madrid, 1757). Since Burriel used Venegas' manuscript of 1739, the work appears under Venegas' name. It was the first book on California to be published.

39. Acrelius, Israel. *A history of New Sweden*...translated from the Swedish...by William M. Reynolds. Philadelphia, Historical Society of Pennsylvania, 1874.

Although the Dutch settlements on the Hudson and the Swedish settlements on the Delaware fell under English domination after 1664, the particular flavor of their respective cultures persisted for several generations. One of the stimulants which prolonged the ethnic life of these areas was the periodic arrival of ministers from the "old country."

In 1749 the Reverend Israel Acrelius was sent out as Provost of the Swedish congregations on the Delaware. His history of New Sweden is the best account of the colony up until his time and gives a primary insight into the process of Americanization. The work first appeared in Swedish in Stockholm in 1759. It was translated into English for the Historical Society of Pennsylvania in 1874 by the Reverend William M. Reynolds.

40. Coxe, William. *Account of the Russian discoveries between Asia and America*...2d. ed. London, Nichols, 1780.

Far less appreciated than our own expansion from east to west across the American continent is the parallel movement west to east across northern Asia by the Russians. During the first half of the 17th century Cossack fur traders swept across Siberia and, during the next hundred years, explored the Asiatic coast and the adjacent islands from China to the Arctic. Beginning in 1720 as part of the cultural revolution of Peter the Great, scientific surveys were sponsored by the Crown and the newly formed Academy of Science. One of the projects was to discover whether a natural land bridge existed between Asia and America.

Between 1725 and 1750 a number of expeditions were launched, most notably those under Vitus Bering. Like so many other explorers of the New World, Bering lost his life in the enterprise. However, the mists which had cloaked the true nature of the icy seas between Asia and America were finally dispelled. The Russians lost no time in exploiting the wealth in furs which the American Pacific coast afforded.

One of the earliest English language accounts of Russian activity in Alaska was provided by William Coxe. Coxe had an opportunity to consult the official journals and confer with various contemporary authorities in St. Petersburg. His work went through two editions in 1780. The copy of the second edition, which we have chosen to reprint, contains corrections and additions as well as a supplement printed in 1787 comparing the voyages of Cook and Clerke with those of the Russians.

41. Bartram, John. *Observations on the inhabitants, climate, soil...* London, Whiston and White, 1751.

John Bartram and Peter Kalm were naturalists. Throughout the middle decades of the 18th century these men—Bartram in the southern back-country and Kalm, the Swedish botanist, in the middle and northern colonies—surveyed, collected, and commented upon the flora and fauna and natural wonders of the New World. This unique little volume links these two men together, and is for the most part a journal by Bartram written while on a trip from Philadelphia to the Onondaga country in western New York.

The trip was undertaken and led by Conrad Weiser, a Palatine pietist, who served as an Indian interpreter for the government of Pennsylvania. At issue was the settling of a dispute between the Six Nations and the colony of Virginia. The ability of the British colonies to maintain friendly relations with the Six Nations through such able agents as Weiser, George Croghan, and Sir William Johnson was the key factor in their ability to threaten the trade lifelines of the French and to compete successfully with them in border areas.

Bartram accompanied Weiser, taking note of the countryside as well as the negotiations with the Indians. The Kalm portion of the book is his account of a trip from the Six Nation country to see the thrilling natural majesty of Niagara Falls. It is the first scientific account of the Falls in English.

42. Washington, George. *The journal of Major George Washington...* London, Jefferys, 1754.

King George's War, which ended in 1748, did little but set the stage for the final clash between France and England. From 1748 to 1754, when the French and Indian War broke out, tension and friction increased all along the border from Maine to Georgia as new posts were constructed and new pressures were applied to the shifting Indian alliances. A critical area of conflict was the Ohio Valley. British traders under the leadership of George Croghan plunged deep into the Ohio country, setting up barter between the Pennsylvania frontiersmen and the Miami, Huron, and Illinois Indians. To cut off this trade the French constructed a string of forts from Lake Erie to the forks of the Ohio in 1753.

The forks of the Ohio, modern Pittsburgh, was the crucial gateway to the Ohio country. Hoping to discourage the French from occupying this strategic point, Governor Dinwiddie of Virginia dispatched Major George Washington to the Ohio River to deliver a warning to the French. The account of this mission, with a copy of the warning and the French reply, was published in *The Journal of Major George Washington* in Williamsburg. It was reprinted in London in 1754, the same year. Washington's mission was unsuccessful; when he returned to the Ohio the following year, the French were busy constructing Fort Duquesne. He was defeated in an engagement and forced to return to Virginia. The last of the colonial wars had begun.

43. Henry, Alexander. *Travels and adventures in Canada and the Indian territories...* New York, Riley, 1809.

The trading opportunities occasioned by the final triumph of England over France in the struggle for empire in America were quickly seized by British entrepreneurs. Merchant-adventurers like Alexander Henry and Peter Pond with their trading connections at Albany transferred their operations to Montreal in 1761 and created the North-West Company. The development of an aggressive Montreal trade resulted in a bitter, sometimes violent, competition with the Hudson's Bay Company, lasting until 1821.

In large measure the vigor and vitality of the Montreal firm

THE DEFEAT OF THE IROQUOIS AT LAKE CHAMPLAIN.
(reduced 17%)
From March Of America Series No. 20

was but an extension of the personalities of its principal managers. Alexander Henry was born in New Jersey in 1743. Arriving at Montreal in 1760 with Amherst's expedition in the capacity of a sutler, he evaluated the trading possibilities being surrendered by the French and was on his way to Fort Michilimackinac—the key emporium of the Great Lakes—within the year. While at Mackinaw he nearly lost his life during Pontiac's uprising. This adventure and many others are recounted in his *Travels and Adventures in Canada* (New York, 1809) which details his activities from 1760 to 1776. Beyond the contributions Henry made toward furthering the trade, both he and Peter Pond were instrumental in promoting exploration of the Canadian West, particularly influencing Alexander MacKenzie's historic overland march to the Pacific.

44. Rogers, Robert. *Journals of Major Robert Rogers*...London, Millan, 1765.

The French and Indian War of 1754 to 1763 had many effects on western settlement. It was the climax in the contest between the French and the English for the thresholds of the interior which had begun with the first colonial war of 1690. The war ended conclusively with England completely dominating Canada and in control of the Ohio Valley. In addition, the war pointed up some distinctive qualities of American personality which had been evolving during the entire colonial experience. Ever since the gentlemen who accompanied John Smith to Virginia had been forced to adapt their ways to prevail over the wilderness, a transformation process of some degree had become the common experience of all immigrants.

One of the best examples of the molding qualities of frontier life is Robert Rogers. Rogers and his Rangers were the guerrillas of the French and Indian War. They were used as scouts and behind enemy lines.

Rogers' *Journal* is primarily an account of their activities; it is also one of the best accounts of the extent of the Americans' adaption of Indian techniques of survival and warfare. The utility of the techniques perfected by Rogers was largely lost on the British.

45. [Smith, William] *An historical account of the expedition against the Ohio Indians*...Philadelphia, Bradford, 1765.

The fury of the Indian uprising of 1763 inspired by Pontiac swept aside all the western posts save Detroit, Fort Pitt, and Fort Niagara. General Amherst responded by ordering relief columns to besiege these forts. A force under Captain Dalyell reached Detroit, and another column under Colonel Bouquet arrived at Fort Pitt after defeating the Indians at Bushy Run. These efforts snuffed out the flickering rebellion. The following year, at a peace conference at Niagara conducted by Sir William Johnson, a general peace accord was reached.

There were a few holdouts. Bouquet was ordered to march from Fort Pitt to the Muskingum Valley in Ohio to pacify the Delawares and Shawnees. The contemporary account of this mission is William Smith's *Historical Account of Bouquet's Expedition* published in Philadelphia in 1765. The march was one of the earliest British military expeditions into the territory northwest of the Ohio River.

46. Morris, Thomas. *Journal of Captain Thomas Morris*...from *Miscellanies in prose and verse*. London, Ridgway, 1791.

This little book contains one of the most fascinating journals relating to the Pontiac uprising. While Colonel Henry Bouquet was marching against the Delawares and Shawnees in southern Ohio in 1764, Colonel John Bradstreet was ordered to take action against the Indians in the northern part of the region along Lake Erie.

He was easily dissuaded from carrying out offensive action by what appeared to be peace overtures by the Indians. At Cedar Point on Lake Erie, Bradstreet detached Captain Thomas Morris to travel through the Indian country to Fort Chartres on the Mississippi. Morris was to obtain assurances of peace from the tribes along the way.

Not far up the Maumee River, Morris and his guide were made prisoners. His journal is the account of efforts to warn Bradstreet of the Indian treachery. The journal was written from notes in a daily diary he kept on the trail. The diary itself was sent back to Bradstreet as a warning. An aide to Bradstreet made a copy of it and returned it to Morris. The original was sent on to General Gage, who was in command of the British Army in America during this period. It is now in the Gage Papers at the Clements Library. Only the journal portion of the 1791 edition has been reproduced for this Series.

47. **[Rickman, John].** *Journal of Captain Cook's last voyage to the Pacific Ocean...*London, Newbery, 1781.

Late in the 18th century Spanish fears for their Pacific coastal claims increased. In the spring of 1778 Captain James Cook appeared off the coast of Oregon and proceeded north to Alaska, searching for the fabled western terminus of the Northwest Passage. Cook, the great navigator and geographer, was a fitting successor to the first Englishman, who had thrown terror into the Spaniards two hundred years before, Francis Drake. Cook, like Drake, circumnavigated the world and sought a sea route through the land mass of North America. This was Cook's third great voyage.

In his first two he had cruised the South Pacific, chasing the mythical and great southern continent. On his third, and last voyage, he scouted the west coast of North America, nosed through the Bering Strait—turning back at the Arctic ice-wall he made his way south—returning to the Hawaiian Islands which he had discovered en route to the American Pacific coast. In Hawaii he was killed by the natives.

One of the earliest accounts of Cook's last voyage was written by one of his officers, John Rickman.

48. **English, William Hayden.** *Conquest of the country northwest of the River Ohio.* Indianapolis, 1896.

The Revolutionary War in the West was largely defensive for the Americans. In the North, Niagara-based Tories and Indian allies terrorized the Mohawk Valley and Detroit-based Henry Hamilton incited the Ohio tribes to cross into the Kentucky settlements. In the South the Indians were so severely defeated by the colonists as to be peaceful.

The growing realization of the need for an aggressive policy in the West provided the support for the proposals of George Rogers Clark. Backed by the colony of Virginia, Clark raised

militiamen and seized control of the Illinois region in 1778. Skill-
fully playing upon the French alliance he won the support of the
French settlers.

Reverses in New York in 1779 and activity by Henry Hamilton, which gave the British the fort of Vincennes, threatened to
undermine all that Clark had gained. By a winter march of great
hardship he surprised Hamilton and took the British garrison.
The account of this march is the subject of Clark's *Memoir*, written at the request of Madison and Jefferson, between 1789 and
1790. It was used by a number of 19th century historians as a
primary source. First published by W. H. English as an appendix
to his *Conquest of the Country Northwest of the River Ohio*
(Indianapolis, 1896), it was also printed in the *George Rogers
Clark Papers* of the Illinois Historical Society in 1912 and by
the Lakeside Press in 1922. For this Series we have used the
1896 W. H. English edition, but only the appendix under the
title of *Clark's Memoir*.

49. Palou, Francisco. *Relacion historica de la vida...Junípero Serra...*
México, Zúñiga y Ontiveros, 1787.

Spanish penetration north from Mexico into Texas and California in the 18th century was inspired by threats of intrusions in
these areas by other imperial powers. The founding of the Louisiana colony by the French alarmed officials in Mexico City who
viewed it as a threat to their influence over the Indian tribes of
the Southwest.

In the California region, the mission work of the Jesuit Fathers
Kino and Salvatierra in the first half of the 18th century was
carried forward by the Franciscans. The pressure of Russian expansion down the coast from Alaska and the fear of imminent
activity by the British on the northern Pacific coast, goaded
Jose de Galvez, the Spanish official in Mexico, to order coastal
and overland expeditions to northern California.

Father Junípero Serra and Gaspar de Portola guided the overland efforts which began in 1769. Within the next fifteen years
a string of setlements stretched from San Diego to San Francisco; nine missions were founded by Father Serra, and California was won for Spain.

The account of Serra's work was recorded by an associate, Father Francisco Palou. The work has been reproduced for this Series from the original Spanish edition printed in Mexico City in 1787.

50. Filson, John. *The discovery, settlement and present state of Kentucke...*Wilmington, Adams, 1784.

The first large-scale migrations into the interior did not proceed directly west, but rather to the south. Large numbers of German and Scotch-Irish immigrants pushed their way west in the mid-1700's as far as the Susquehanna and then were deflected south into the Shenandoah by the mountain and Indian barriers. With the end of the French and Indian War, the Indian threat was temporarily removed and land company lobbyists were successful in having large tracts of the interior opened to settlement.

Daniel Boone's family was one of those who had moved from Pennsylvania down the great valleys of Appalachia. Boone himself was raised in Yadkin Valley in North Carolina. After the French and Indian War he was lured west by tales of the Kentucky country. Boone was not the first frontiersman through the Cumberland Gap, but he ranged more widely over that "dark and bloody ground" than any previous white man.

Backing Boone's activity was the wealthy Carolina speculator, Judge Richard Henderson. Taking advantage of the outcome of Lord Dunmore's war with the Shawnees in 1774, Henderson negotiated the purchase of a large section of Kentucky for his Transylvania Company and employed Boone to open a road to the region.

The story of Daniel Boone's contribution to opening Kentucky was recorded in John Filson's *The Discovery, Settlement and present State of Kentucke* (Wilmington 1784). Filson, himself, went to Kentucky sometime in 1782 or 1783. His description of the land and its potentials precedes the account of Boone. It is the earliest history of Kentucky.

51. [Cutler, Manasseh] *An explanation of the map which delineates that part of the federal lands...*Salem, Dabney and Cushing, 1787.

The Revolution accomplished more than independence from

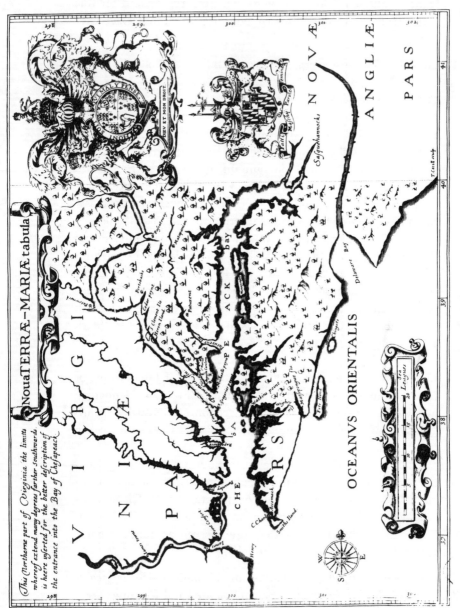

MAP OF MARYLAND.
(reduced 23%)
From March Of America Series No. 22

Great Britain; it won the right for the United States to develop the West. For the new republic it was a right fraught with as much peril as possibility. The questions of land policy, self-determination, and Indian relations remained as much a problem for the United States as they had been for the powerful British Empire.

The first step was to gain jurisdiction over the western lands, so the states were badgered into ceding their western claims to the new Federal Government. Next, two ordinances were passed: the first in 1785 set up procedures for surveying, so that land could be sold in an organized fashion with a minimum of dispute, and the second in 1787 laid down the manner in which the territories were to be governed and come into the Union equally wth the old states, a problem the British had never solved.

Amidst all the natural difficulties attending the establishment of the land policy there were various interest groups—veterans, land companies, speculators, and merchant-traders—all pressing their claims and trying to gain a friendly ear in Congress. One of the most successful operators was the Reverend Manassah Cutler. Cutler represented the Ohio Company, formed in Boston in 1786 by General Tupper and General Putnam. These men sold shares in the company to veterans in exchange for land warrants which they had received for their military service. Cutler petitioned Congress for one-and-a-half million acres along the Ohio River at 66 cents an acre. To obtain this grant he acted as a front man for a group of legislators and officials who had formed the Scioto Land Company. Cutler combined the requests of both companies successfully.

Cutler produced a map and a description of the lands to induce settlement in 1787. In 1788 the town of Marietta was founded by settlers of the Ohio Company. Cutler's *Guide to the Federal Lands* is a very rare item. The particular copy reproduced for this Series belonged to Winthrop Sargent, a partner of Cutler and secretary of the Northwest Territory, later first governor of the Southwest Territory.

52. **Mackenzie, Sir Alexander.** *Voyages from Montreal, on the river St. Laurence...*London, Cadell and Davies, 1801.

While the French and Indian War ended the trade rivalry between the French and the British, various trading companies under British management soon fell into bitter competition among themselves. One of the best examples is the scramble between the Hudson's Bay Company and the North West Company at Montreal for the trade of the western tribes. No small consequence of this trade activity were the explorations of men like Samuel Hearne and Alexander Mackenzie. Hearne corroborated by land exploration Cook's findings that there was indeed no Strait of Anian from Hudson Bay to the Pacific. Mackenzie was the first to reach the northwest Pacific coast by an overland route.

Supported by the preliminary work of Peter Pond and Alexander Henry, Mackenzie accomplished an amazing survey of northwest Canada, exploring the Mackenzie River north to the Arctic in 1789 and reaching the shore of the Pacific in 1793. The account of these feats appeared in his *Voyages from Montreal...* (London, 1801).

53. **Spencer, Oliver M.** *Indian captivity...* New York, Waugh and Mason, 1835.

Although Congress was successful in solving the physical problems of marking off the new territories and setting up the administrative machinery in 1785 and 1787, the problems of actually building homesteads and, particularly, of removing the Indians still lay ahead. With the active backing of the British commanders, who still held the forts of the Northwest, the Indians stiffened their resistance to ceding any more land to the United States. The government agents, accepting agreements from any portion of a tribe as binding for the entire tribe, pressed for Indian removal. By 1789 the Ohio country was on the verge of war.

In 1790 and 1791 two successive military expeditions, one under Josiah Harmar and the other under Arthur St. Clair, were defeated by the Indians. Emboldened by their victories, the Indians threatened to roll back the northern frontier. It was in this time of uncertainty on the frontier, 1792—two years before Anthony Wayne would defeat the Indians at Fallen Timbers— that the captivity of Oliver Spencer took place.

Oliver Spencer, Jr. was about nine years old in 1790 when his father, Colonel Oliver Spencer, set out from New Jersey to join with other Jerseymen in settling the town of Columbia on the Ohio River near what was to become Cincinnati. The account of young Oliver's captivity was written years later when he was a Methodist minister, yet the events of 1792 seem to have been engraved on his memory. The account appeared in 1834 in the Methodist magazine, "The Western Christian Advocate" and was published in book form the following year. At least twelve editions came off the press before the Civil War. It reads like the adventures of an early Boy Scout.

54. McAfee, Robert Breckinridge. *History of the late war in the western country.* Lexington, Ky., Worsley & Smith, 1816.

Although the conflicts between the settlers and the Indians in the Northwest Territory were frequently abated in the 1790's, the central issues remained unresolved. The westward flow of settlers and the Indian intrigues of the British continued. At least as far as the West was concerned, then, some major clash was inevitable; it occurred in the form of the War of 1812.

Of the three major sectors of the War of 1812—the eastern seaboard, the Canadian–New York border, and the West—only in the West did the British suffer a genuine setback. Not only were they forced to relinquish forts they held, but their hope of establishing an Indian buffer state which would have parried the westward thrust of the Americans was dashed. The Indians themselves, deprived of their British allies and bereft of the warrior-statesman, Tecumseh, were doomed to be uprooted and driven across the Mississippi. Robert McAfee's *History of the Late War in the Western Country* (Lexington, 1816) related the western campaign from Tippecanoe to New Orleans. Having access to the papers of General William Henry Harrison and General Isaac Shelby of Kentucky, he was able to describe with accuracy those aspects of the war he had not witnessed as an American officer.

55. Bishop, Abraham. *Georgia speculation unveiled.* Hartford, Babcock, 1797-1798. 2 v.

International intrigue, Indian unrest, high finance, low politics, and a Supreme Court decision all contributed to the story of the Yazoo land grants. The Yazoo country made up most of the present states of Alabama and Mississippi. Instead of ceding these western lands to the Federal Government as its sister states did, the state of Georgia tried to bolster its sagging, post-Revolutionary War economy by selling tracts of the Yazoo country. Despite the questionable nature of the claim—Spain disputed the lower section as part of West Florida, and the Indians disputed all claims—the Georgia Legislature made grants on two occasions (1789, 1795) to groups of speculators. The first venture soured, and the second group of companies had its grant cancelled by the legislature of 1796.

These Georgia lawmakers had been swept into office on a wave of protest against land "give-aways" and legislative "payoffs." The cry of "fraud" went up from the thousands of people who had bought land warrants from the companies. A flurry of pamphlets appeared, some warning the public to beware of worthless warrants, others attacking or defending the speculators and the legislators. One of the best warnings was issued by Abraham Bishop in his *Georgia Speculation Unveiled* (Hartford, 1797). Bishop, a New Englander, addressed himself to his fellow northerners, many of whom had bought heavily at low prices, hoping to turn pennies into dollars in reselling the warrants.

The speculators appealed to the Federal Government on the Constitutional basis that the Georgia Legislature had broken a contract. The lands were ceded to the United States in 1802. In 1810 the Supreme Court ruled in *Fletcher* v. *Peck* that the Georgia Legislature had indeed violated a contract when it cancelled the 1795 sales. Compensation was finally voted the warrant holders in 1814 by the U.S. Congress.

56. Lewis, Meriwether. *History of the expedition under the command of Captains Lewis and Clark…* by Paul Allen. Philadelphia, Bradford and Inskeep, 1814. 2 v.

Thomas Jefferson had a scientific and nationalistic interest in the

West long before he had the opportunity to buy Louisiana from Napoleon in 1803. In 1786 he had encouraged the wanderer, John Ledyard, to hike through the West; in 1792 he urged the American Philosophical Society to underwrite an expedition. Finally in 1803, prior to the Louisiana Purchase, he secured a secret appropriation from Congress to finance an exploring party. The subsequent trek of Meriwether Lewis and William Clark (1804-1806) is one of the most famous in our history. Not only did they accomplish the first ascent of the Missouri River and travel overland through the Rockies to the Columbia River and the Pacific coast, but they formed the first really scientific western expedition. As a government financed and supervised effort this expedition represented a continuing national interest in the development of the West. Their march underscored the magnitude of the continent's width, something which had often been miscalculated previously. They also filled in the details about the varied topography, as well as calling attention to at least five passes through the mountains.

Beginning in 1806 various accounts and summaries of their trip began to appear, mostly in newspapers. In 1807 Patrick Gass, a member of the party, published his journal. This journal and some of the newspaper accounts were used for an edition of *The Travels of Capt. Lewis & Clark*...published in Philadelphia in 1809. The "Biddle" edition which appeared in 1814, considered to be the best of the early editions, was the one used for this Series.

57. **Pike, Zebulon Montgomery.** *An account of expeditions to the sources of the Mississippi*...Philadelphia, Conrad, 1810.

Thomas Jefferson's inquiry into the nature of the newly purchased Louisiana Territory did not stop with the expedition of Lewis and Clark. Among others who were sent out on expeditions in the years following was Zebulon M. Pike. Pike was a twenty-six-year-old lieutenant when he was dispatched by General James Wilkinson in 1805 to explore the sources of the Mississippi. Starting from St. Louis he took a keelboat up-river into Minnesota.

Indian Wheat

An Indian Iay

FRONTISPIECE.
(original size)
From March Of America Series No. 24

In 1806 and 1807 he led a march west through Missouri, Kansas, Colorado, south into New Mexico and Mexico, and then east through Texas to Louisiana. On his southward journey he probed deep into Spanish territory and was escorted to the Louisiana border under guard. Although his papers and maps were taken from him by the Spaniards, he was able to remember enough of the southwest border to write a convincing report. This, along with an account of his previous exploit, was published in 1810.

58. Ross, Alexander. *Adventures of the first settlers on the Oregon or Columbia river...*London, Smith, Elder, 1849.

Hardly had Lewis and Clark returned from their trip up the Missouri before other white men were on their way to the Oregon country. The frontier, skirmish line here was formed as it had been elsewhere by hunters and traders. These outriders of civilization continued to vie with the government geographers for being first in a region.

In the case of Oregon it was the Pacific Fur Company of John Jacob Astor which was first. Hoping to compete with the Hudson's Bay and North West Companies for the furs of the Pacific coast, and to open a wedge in the China trade, Astor set up the post of Astoria on the Columbia River in 1810. This post was to be supplied by sea and to be linked overland with St. Louis.

The story of this venture is told by Alexander Ross, one of the participants. Ross was a native of Scotland who migrated to Canada and served as a clerk for Astor. Later he returned to Canada as an employee of another trading company.

59. Bradbury, John. *Travels in the interior of America, in the years 1809, 1810 and 1811...*Liverpool, Smith and Galway, 1817.

John Bradbury, a Scotsman living in England, was commissioned by the Botanical Society of Liverpool to gather botanical information on the American interior. Arriving in America with an introduction to Thomas Jefferson, he was advised by Jefferson to make his headquarters at St. Louis rather than at New Orleans.

At St. Louis Bradbury signed on a party preparing to go up the Missouri. This was the overland group of Astorian fur traders

under the leadership of Wilson Price Hunt. Bradbury accompanied them as far as the Arikara villages. Later he traveled further into the Mandan country. He returned downstream with
another traveler, Henry M. Brackenridge.

Bradbury's account is of more than just botanical interest; he
was an astute observer and fearless frontiersman in his own
right. Following his trip up the Missouri, he went to New Orleans and then to New York. Prevented from returning to England during the War of 1812, he remained in America, traveling
through most of the Midwest. His insight and reflections in this
portion of his work, which appears in the appendix, is of as
much interest as his trip up the Missouri. The book first appeared in Liverpool in 1817; a second edition was printed in
1819. The copy of the first edition used in this Series was obtained from the Rare Book Room of the General Library of the
University of Michigan.

60. Brackenridge, Henry Marie. *Views of Louisiana*...Pittsburgh, Cramer, Spear and Eichbaum, 1814.

When John Jacob Astor set up his trading post for the Pacific
Fur Company on the Columbia River in 1811, the initial settlement was built by a party brought to the Pacific coast by ship.
Another group under the leadership of Wilson Price Hunt set
out from St. Louis to follow Lewis and Clark's overland route up
the Missouri to the Columbia. Among the members of this expedition was John Bradbury, the British botanist. Three weeks
later a second party of traders left St. Louis to warn them of
increasing Indian danger. This party, led by the trader Manuel
Lisa, included a young lawyer, Henry M. Brackenridge. They
overtook the Hunt party near the Mandan villages. Leaving the
traders to proceed to Oregon, Bradbury and Brackenridge toured
the country on their way back to St. Louis.

Brackenridge's journal of the trip up the Missouri first appeared with his *Views of Louisiana* in 1814. It was revised and
published separately in 1815 and 1816. The early edition has
been republished for this Series.

61. [Cramer, Zadok]. *The navigator...*8th edition. Pittsburgh, Cramer, Spear and Eichbaum, 1814.

Today when Americans travel they can get a strip map from the local automobile association which has on successive pages a suggested route, places to see, places to spend the night, and an assortment of warnings and advice. The process for putting these guides together may be more streamlined, but the general concept has changed very little since Zadok Cramer issued his first *Navigator* in Pittsburgh in 1801 for travelers preparing to embark on a westward trip down the Ohio River.

By 1824 the *Navigator* had gone through twelve editions. There are very few copies of the earliest editions in existence; they were used until they fell apart. Additional testimony to the utility of this work is the great number of imitators it inspired. The 8th edition, printed in 1814, was selected for this series since it was this edition which was carried by many of the settlers who took part in the flood of migration which surged west after the War of 1812.

62. Birkbeck, Morris. *Notes on a journey in America, from the coast of Virginia to the territory of Illinois.* 4th edition. London, Severn, 1818.

During the decade following the close of the War of 1812, the Great Lakes plains, western Ohio, Indiana, Illinois, and finally southern Michigan experienced the first heavy wave of western migration. Often the migration produced whole towns over night or took the form of a colony settled by a group of immigrants from Europe. The latter was the case for the English Prairie in Edwards County, Illinois.

Organized by Morris Birkbeck and George Flower for agriculturally distressed farmers in England, the colony attracted many settlers in the years following 1818. One of the reasons for its attraction was the promotional activities of Birkbeck. His *Notes on a Journey from Virginia to Illinois* and his *Letters from Illinois* went through several editions in 1818 and 1819 in in America, London, and Dublin. A London edition of 1818 was used for this Series.

63. Nuttall, Thomas. *A journal of travels into the Arkansa territory, during the year 1819*...Philadelphia, Palmer, 1821.

> Thomas Nuttall, like John Bradbury, was a young Englishman interested in botany and exploration. Arriving in Philadelphia in 1808, at the age of twenty-two, he was in St. Louis two years later with Bradbury. He spent the next few years along the east coast and returned to the West in 1818. His journal recounts his travel experiences from Philadelphia to the Arkansas River. Although his interest was centered upon scientific observation, his account provides an eyewitness record of life and conditions on the lower Mississippi at the time when western migration was starting to cross over. In 1819 Arkansas was made a separate territory from Missouri.

64. Wright, John Stillman. *Letters from the West; or a caution to emigrants*...Salem, N. Y., Dodd & Stevenson, 1819.

> The land boom which resulted in the filling up of the Old Northwest after the War of 1812 was more than just a result of economic conditions; it took on some of the aspects of mob hysteria. John S. Wright of Washington County, New York was infected by this "Ohio mania," but had the good sense to scout out the "western paradise" before moving his family.
>
> In a series of letters home to friends he describes his disillusionment with the exaggerations of the land companies. While at times he appears bitter at these distortions, his comment is not all unfavorable. His trip took him down the Ohio River as far as Illinois. He returned by way of Cleveland, noting some of the pleasant aspects of the Connecticut Western Reserve region. The book provides some insight as to why men moved west and what they were apt to find.

65. James, Edwin, comp. *Account of an expedition from Pittsburgh to the Rocky mountains...under the command of Major Stephen H. Long*...Philadelphia, Carey and Lea, 1822-1823. 2 v.

> A decade passed after Pike's expedition in 1805, 1806, and 1807 before the national government sponsored another party. Although destined to be a series of failures and blunders the exploration conducted by Major Stephen H. Long was not without

value or enduring effects. Begun originally in 1818 as an effort to plant military posts on the upper Missouri to protect the fur trade, control the Indians, and circumscribe the influence of the British companies, the project never got off the ground.

The next year, 1819, Secretary of War John C. Calhoun instructed Major Long to conduct an investigation of the sources of the Platte River and to return by way of the Red River and the Arkansas. The account of this adventure was written by one of the party, Edwin James. Aside from losing its way and most of its records, the expedition was the first actually to climb Pike's Peak in Colorado. Its less than enthusiastic report of the southwest and the maps which showed a "Great American Desert" discouraged migration in the region for many years.

66. **Schoolcraft, Henry Rowe.** *Narrative journal of travels through the northwestern regions of the United States...in the year 1820...* Albany, Hosford, 1821.

The first wave of immigration into the old Northwest following the War of 1812 passed by Michigan, choosing instead Indiana and Illinois. Partly responsible for this was the poor publicity gained from superficial survey reports which described the land as swampy and the climate unhealthy. Not one to permit such a slander to stand unchallenged, Lewis Cass, Governor of Michigan and Indian Superintendent of the territory—including Wisconsin and part of Minnesota—proposed an expedition to the War Department in 1819 which would ostensibly establish better relations with the western tribes, but would also serve as a scientific foray to note and advertise the potential of Michigan.

Cass obtained the mineralogical services of Henry P. Schoolcraft. Schoolcraft had just won a national reputation for his work describing mining in Missouri. The expedition left Detroit in the spring of 1820 and returned in the fall, covering 4,000 miles in 122 days. Schoolcraft's account which was published in 1821 received widespread notice and turned attention toward Michigan.

67. **Pattie, James Ohio.** *The personal narrative of James O. Pattie of Kentucky...*edited by Timothy Flint. Cincinnati, Flint, 1833.

The family odyssey of James O. Pattie was typical of many early

CROSSING OF PLATTE MOUTH OF DEER CREEK.
(original size)
From March of America Series No. 88

American families. His grandfather had been born in Virginia and moved to Kentucky during the Revolution, his father had left Kentucky and gone to Missouri, where he took part in the War of 1812. Pattie accompanied his father across the plains to Santa Fe, New Mexico, where they became involved in the fur trade. He lived and traveled through the Spanish Southwest and California from 1824-1830.

Although some historians have questioned his ability to recall precisely the amazing events of his wanderings which he recounted to Timothy Flint, his work reflects the attitudes of Anglo-American "gringos" toward the Spaniards. More importantly he was a member of one of the earliest trading parties to use the Santa Fe Trail.

68. Stewart, Catherine. *New homes in the West.* Nashville, Cameron and Fall, 1843.

The development of the West involved more than just the removal of the Indians from the land, or building settlements and planting farms in a wilderness. It was a complex process of men affecting environment and in turn being affected by it. The successful outcome of the War of 1812 enabled Americans to turn their backs on Europe for almost a century and indulge themselves in expansion and internal affairs. This isolationism and the great job of pushing back the frontier inspired a host of notions about what they were doing and its significance in the history of man.

Americans came to think of their role in history as unique, a modern chosen people. Their West was a new Eden where the precepts of freedom and Christianity mixed with the purity of the untouched land, where the land's goodness and a boundless horizon marked the new day of a new people. The chauvinism of manifest destiny, the canonization of agriculture, and the conferring of nobility upon the savage were all a part of the mixture of nationalism and romanticism of the first half of the nineteenth century. Foreign travelers observed this, but nowhere was it more evident than in the writings of Americans themselves. Catherine Stewart's *New Homes in the West* captures this optimistic spirit. Dismissed are the dreary Puritan images of the foreboding forest primeval, the rugged Zion in the wilderness. The wilderness has been transformed from a place of jeopardy to a place of security. Virtue, education, and industry are no longer associated exclusively with urban civilization, but to the contrary they are the singular attributes of the frontier. Catherine Stewart's work reflects these assumptions in her descriptions of life in the Great Lakes area during the 1830's.

69. Leonard, Zenas. *Narrative of the adventures of Zenas Leonard...* Clearfield, Pa., Moore, 1839.

During the years 1831 to 1835 Zenas Leonard lived the life of a mountain man. This extinct breed of fur trapper and trader roamed the far western fringes of American settlement, often adding more to our knowledge of the physical character of the West than to his own pocket. Born in west central Pennsylvania, Leonard left home early to pursue the Rocky Mountain fur trade. While in the West he participated in Joseph Walker's expedition to California, the first party to reach the Pacific by way of the Sierra Nevada Mountains. Both Leonard and Walker were in the general employ of Captain B. L. E. Bonneville, a U. S. military officer on leave, who was engaging in the fur trade.

Leonard's narrative was first published by the Clearfield, Pennsylvania *Republican* in book form in 1839. It is one of the fundamental sources for the exploration of the American West.

70. *A visit to Texas: being the journal of a traveller...* New York, Goodrich & Wiley, 1834.

The migration to Texas in the 1820's was the logical extension of the impulse which began in Tennessee and rolled through Missouri, Arkansas, and Louisiana. Although trading contacts had existed between Mexicans in Texas and Anglo-Americans since 1800, it was almost twenty-five years later an Anglo-American settlement in Texas was opened by Moses and Stephen Austin. From the outset the Mexican government stipulated that newcomers must be members of the Roman Catholic Church and accept the responsibility of Mexican citizenship. These qualifications were enforced unevenly. The migration itself was uneven; squatters had already filtered into the northeastern corner of the state. Other individuals followed Austin's lead and applied as *empresarios* for grants to which they would conduct new settlers.

In 1830 some of these *empresarios* sold their claims to Boston and New York financiers who formed the Galveston Bay and Texas Land Company. The company owned no land; what it owned was the right to settle land reserved by the grants or claims. The settlers would still have to buy the land from the Mexican land office. The company, however, sold the right to settle in the form of company scrip. Many people thought this was equivalent to gaining title to the land. One of those to discover he had been misled was an anonymous New Yorker who went to Texas in 1831. His *Visit to Texas* is one of the earliest accounts of the settlement of the region along the Brazos River. It both praised the potential for development and warned prospective immigrants of the fraudulent character of the company's promotional campaign.

71. Gregg, Josiah. *Commerce of the prairies: or, The Journal of a Santa Fé trader*...New York, Langley, 1844. 2 v.

Josiah Gregg, Santa Fe trader, explorer, geographer, naturalist, storekeeper, doctor, lawyer, surveyor, war correspondent, and author left us a rich, readable account of the southwest trade between 1831 and 1840. Although it was not the first such account, it was one of the best because of the wide-ranging interests of the author.

Born in Overton County, Tennessee in 1806, Gregg moved with his family to Illinois and then to Missouri. Sickly and shy, he was rebuffed in his early attempts to study medicine and law. In an effort to improve his health he signed with a merchant caravan on its way from Independence, Missouri to Santa Fe, New Mexico in 1831. For the next nine years he crossed and recrossed the plains four times. Although he went on to serve as a correspondent in the Mexican War, made contributions in the field of botany, and explored supply routes for California miners, his *Commerce of the Prairies* is a most lasting contribution to our knowledge of the West.

72. Wyeth, John B. *Oregon; or, A short history of a long journey from the Atlantic Ocean to the region of the Pacific by land...* Cambridge, Wyeth, 1833.

When John Jacob Astor's Pacific Fur Company on the Columbia River in Oregon failed (1811-1813), the trading activity in the Pacific Northwest was forfeited to the Canadian Hudson's Bay Company, which became the dominant enterprise in the region. By 1830, however, the Rocky Mountain Fur Company began to exploit the central Rockies and probe towards Oregon. Under its auspices the famous "rendezvous system" was established with trappers coming in at an appointed time to a predetermined place to meet and exchange their furs for supplies with a Missouri merchant caravan.

In 1832 Captain Nathanial J. Wyeth had attached himself and his party to one of these caravans as it wended its way toward the rendezvous. Wyeth, a native of New England, had been inspired by an Oregon enthusiast and colonization promoter Hall J. Kelley. Hoping to establish a settlement, Wyeth sent a ship around the Horn and made his way overland with a small group of supporters. Before reaching Oregon where he was to learn of the loss of his ship, his party lost most of its members through desertion. One of those who turned back was his cousin, John B. Wyeth. The account John wrote on his return cooled some of the heated excitement about Oregon, but its effect was temporary. Nathaniel made a second attempt which was more successful, and the trail to Oregon was soon crowded with wagon trains replacing the trading caravans.

73. Griffiths, D., jr. *Two years' residence in the new settlements of Ohio...* London, Westley and Davis, 1835.

Large scale settlement began in Ohio after 1795 when Wayne's Treaty of Greeneville removed the Indians from much of the territory. The various land companies conducted settlers down the Ohio River and up the river valleys which fed it. About the same time the Western Reserve which lay along the shores of Lake Erie and had previously belonged to Connecticut was opened to settlement. Nearly all the settlers who came there in the ensuing migration were from New England. The towns which sprang up reflected much of the New England character; their architecture, their village greens, and their Puritan outlook.

From 1832 to 1834 D. Griffiths, an Englishman, visited the settlements in the Western Reserve. The purpose of his account of his visit was to instruct English immigrants in how to go about coming to the New World. In a very readable and enjoyable way he combines instruction, reflection, and description—discussing such things as the sea voyage from England to America, the trip on the Erie Canal, and life in the wilderness. Particularly interesting are his insights into the American attitudes on slavery, temperance, and religion.

74. **Nowlin, William.** *The bark covered house, or Back in the woods again*...Detroit, 1876.

Although the traders and trappers were ranging as far west as the Rockies by the mid 1830's, the mainstream of westward movement was still pushing through the Mississippi Valley. In 1834 John Nowlin moved his family west from Putman County, New York to Michigan. High land prices in New York and the growing scarcity of land were the chief reasons for his move west. A trip across country to Utica, on the Erie Canal, and a boat ride from Buffalo to Detroit carried the family to its new home in the wilderness. The story in this pioneer family is recounted by the son, William Nowlin, in *The Bark Covered House*. Now quite a rarity, the work presents a typical picture of life in the early settlements.

75. **Hoffman, Charles Fenno.** *A winter in the West. By a New-Yorker* ...New York, Harper, 1835. 2 v.

Something of the charm of the midwestern wilderness is captured in Charles Fenno Hoffman's *A Winter in the West*. A novelist and editor of the "Knickerbocker Magazine," he traveled in 1833 from New York to Pittsburgh to Cleveland, then by boat to Detroit, and by horseback to Chicago, visiting Wisconsin, Minnesota, St. Louis, and returning by way of Kentucky and Virginia. No doubt some of the inspiration for the glowing praise Hoffman heaped on the West was his desire to counter the

THE INDIAN PONY.
(original size)
From March Of America Series No. 99

criticism flowing from the pens of various English travelers. Some of these wanderers were justly picqued at the distortions of the promotional literature and the downright crude conditions which confronted them. Others had discovered that there was money to be made from books that "plucked the Eagle's feathers." Hoffman's account offers one of the best views of early Chicago.

76. [Ingraham, Joseph Holt]. *The South-west. By a Yankee...*New York, Harper, 1835. 2 v.

Although Mississippi was made a territory in 1798 it was not until after the War of 1812 that it experienced its first large-scale immigration. In the years following the war settlers from the southern Atlantic coastal states moved west in droves. Spurred on by worn-out eastern lands and the promise of quick wealth from new technological developments which made upland cotton practical, they took advantage of the recent Indian treaties opening rich lands and rode the wave of general postwar prosperity.

A second period of growth occurred in the 1830's by which time the plantation system was thoroughly entrenched. *The South-West. By a Yankee* contains the observations of Joseph Holt Ingraham, a native of Portland, Maine who went to Mississippi about 1830 to teach college. The first volume reports on life in New Orleans and the second on Natchez. Ingraham was mildly apologetic of slavery and generally amenable to Southern life.

77. [Potter, Woodburne]. *The war in Florida...By a late staff Officer.* Baltimore, Lewis and Coleman, 1836.

The incessant displacement of the Indians was a historic act of conquest even by the opening of the 19th century. Beginning with the War of 1812, however, it proceeded at a ferocious pace; William Henry Harrison being the leading figure in the old Northwest and Andrew Jackson in the South. Throughout the 1820's one southern tribe after another—Creeks, Chickasaws, Choctaws, and finally the Cherokees—were uprooted and packed-off to Arkansas. Only the Seminoles held out.

The Seminoles were originally a breakaway faction of the Creeks who migrated to Florida in the mid-18th century. When the United States finally obtained Florida from Spain in 1821 after years of border warfare, the Seminoles were assigned a large reservation north of Lake Okeechobee. By 1833, however, this sanctuary had become both a temptation and a threat to the growing plantation economy. New land, even the watery world of the Everglades was coveted; moreover as long as the Seminoles remained, they provided a haven for runaway slaves. The attempts to get them to leave are a catalogue of trickery and bad faith. The warfare which resulted from their refusal to be moved flared and flickered until 1842. The U.S. Army had to relearn all of the skills of guerrilla warfare it had forgotten since the day of Robert Rogers.

One of the best accounts of the Seminole War is Woodburne Potter's *The War in Florida*. Equally divided between the causes and events of the war, the work expresses some of the shame and chagrin felt by the soldiers who did their duty. It also conveys their disgust with unscrupulous Indian agents and slave-catchers.

78. Kendall, George Wilkins. *Narrative of an expedition across the great southwestern prairies, from Texas to Santa Fé...*London, Bogue, 1845.

Westward expansion, while accomplishing astounding growth for the country and securing for it a place as world power, was not without its less ennobling aspects, particularly as it affected Americans' ideas about themselves. Successive conquests and unbounded horizons inspired distorted and unfounded notions of invincibility and righteousness. Expansion abetted usurpation and greed, a sense of uniqueness and of manifest destiny. It is not surprising therefore to find many examples of so called "liberating" expeditions, groups of free-booters or "filibusters," partly inspired by greed, partly by a nationalistic zeal. Most of these expeditions were launched against the Spanish holdings of the South and West.

One such enterprise was the attempt by the Lone Star Republic of Texas to liberate the territory of New Mexico in 1841. Not only would the people of Santa Fe to be permitted the fruits of freedom, but the Texas republic would be enriched incidentally by the trade with New Mexico, then being enjoyed by Missouri. George Wilkins Kendall, who wrote the account of the expedition was a printer by trade. Arriving in New Orleans from New York in 1833 he founded the New Orleans *Picayune* in 1837. In 1841 he was invited to join the effort against Santa Fe. His account first appeared in the columns of his newspaper; it is well-written and reveals as much about life in the Southwest as it does about the predatory patriotism of the Southwestern leaders.

79. Frémont, John Charles. *Report of the exploring expedition to the Rocky mountains in the year 1842, and to Oregon and north California in the years 1843—'44.* Washington, Gales and Seaton, 1845.

By the early 1840's the idea of expanding to the continental limits to achieve America's "manifest destiny" had won supporters both within and outside of Congress. Senators such as Thomas Hart Benton of Missouri and John B. Floyd of Virginia had taken up the cause of the Oregon enthusiasts. Of no small benefit to this cause was the creation of the Corps of Topographical Engineers in 1838. Partly in response to the climate created by the expansionists and partly in the tradition which dated back to Thomas Jefferson, the topographical engineers had the job of mapping the West and gathering scientific information. The goals of manifest destiny and the activity of the engineers were soon united in the person of John C. Frémont. A son-in-law to Senator Benton and a captain in the engineers, Frémont engaged in five expeditions between 1842 and 1853. Of these, the first two were influential to settlement.

His first journey in 1842 took him up the Platt River and through the South Pass of the Rockies to the Wind River range. While he gathered a great deal of scientific data, his main purpose and that of Senator Benton was to find the quickest and safest way for immigrants to get to Oregon. On his second expedition in 1843 and 1844 he completed a survey of the Oregon trail, begun by a naval expedition up the Columbia River, then swung south in a great arc which took him through the great basin of the Salt Lake, over the mountains into California, down the Valley of California, and east through Utah, Colorado, Kansas and Missouri. Although his scientific findings provided much information about the Great Basin region, these revelations were minor in effect, compared with the romantic impact of his report. Frémont succeeded in dramatizing the sheer awe of the majestic West, the patriotic zest of a western empire. He wrote about mountain men such as Kit Carson. His report was influential in directing the Mormons toward Salt Lake.

80. Scott, James Leander. *A journal of a missionary tour through Pennsylvania, Ohio, Indiana*...Providence, 1843.

Traditional institutions of society such as churches and schools were often left behind in the dust of the western movement. When the churches did try to catch-up with the march of settlers, it was often the newer denominations which gained a following in the backcountry. Lacking form and orthodoxy, they had a natural appeal in the unstructured West. During the mid-19th century those churches which had been fused in the white heat of the revival impulse were impelled to carry their message to the wilderness, eschewing slavery, trumpeting temperance, and warning against other forms of worship, usually Mormonism and Roman Catholicism. Missionaries were often sent as advance agents to seek areas where a systematic effort might bring the most results. James Scott's *Journal of a Missionary Tour* is a record of such a trip in 1842. Blinded to all viewpoints except his own, his description of the countryside is however quite detached and informative. Particularly good are his remarks about early settlement in Iowa.

81. Oliver, William. *Eight months in Illinois*...Newcastle-upon-Tyne, Mitchell, 1843.

When the settlers moved into the Midwest in the years following the War of 1812, they first sought-out the rich bottom lands along the rivers and streams. Next in preference were the upland forests, and lastly the prairies. The reluctance to farm the prairie was occasioned partly by myth and partly by method. To men who had lived and worked all their lives in forests, there was something unnerving about a vast treeless plain. But more important, to men accustomed to building their cabins, farm buildings, and furniture out of wood, the dearth of trees on the prairie posed very real problems. Moreover, to break the hard prairie sod, capital had to be accumulated to purchase heavy plows. Wells had to be dug, farm animals had to be purchased, and still the prairie farmer had to face the harsh, swift violence of nature.

By the early 1840's, when William Oliver went to Illinois, the Midwest had filled-up to the point where the prairies were all that were left unsettled. Oliver, like Morris Birkbeck before him, was interested in locating suitable farming areas for depressed laborers and farmers from England. Witty and perceptive, his account of Illinois and his admonition to immigrants is one of the best.

82. Johnson, Overton. *Route across the Rocky mountains, with a description of Oregon and California...by Overton Johnson and Wm. H. Winter.* Lafayette, Ind., Semans, 1846.

Although the Oregon enthusiast, Nathaniel J. Wyeth, had established a settlement as early as 1833, and "mountain men," missionaries and army surveyors came to the territory in the following years, it was not until 1843 that large-scale migration took place. It was this "Great Migration" that insured American interest in the territory. In May of that year, more than a thousand settlers left Independence, Missouri alone.

A variety of circumstances were responsible for the assembling of such a large party: enthusiastic reports from the mission posts in the Willamette valley, depressed economic conditions in the Midwest, and simply the "Oregon Fever." The leader of the party was Peter H. Burnett, who had spent the previous season lecturing on Oregon throughout western Missouri. Whether it was these lectures or a prior decision that led two Indiana college boys to join the wagon train is not known, but their account of the migration and subsequent trip to California is a first-rate work.

Overton Johnson and William H. Winter had both attended Wabash College, intermittently, in the late 1830's. Winter was in Missouri by 1841 and was visited there by Johnson. A little

more than a year later they joined Burnett's group at Independence. Upon reaching Willamette Falls, Winter separated from
the main party and accompanied a group to California. Returning, he gave his notes to Johnson, who used them in publishing
a full acount of the expedition.

83. Palmer, Joel. *Journal of travels over the Rocky mountains, to the*
mouth of the Columbia river... Cincinnati, James, 1847.

The tide of overland immigration which engulfed Oregon in
1843 was followed by even larger waves in subsequent years.
The 1845 migration doubled the population of the territory. Out
of this experience came one of the most complete accounts of
wagon train life, Joel Palmer's *Journal of Travels Over the*
Rocky Mountains. Published first in 1847, it went through two
more editions, in 1851 and 1852, because it was useful as a
guide for immigrants.

Palmer was born of Quaker parents in Canada in 1810. When
the War of 1812 broke out the family moved back to their native
state of New York. At the age of sixteen Palmer was in Bucks
County, Pennsylvania where he learned something about canal
building. Ten years later in 1836 he was building canals in Indiana. He served a term in the Indiana legislature and went west
in 1845.

Returning home to Indiana for his family in 1846, he wrote
his book and waited impatiently for its delayed printing. He
obtained only a dozen copies before setting out again the next
year for Oregon. There he served as quartermaster and com-
missary general in the Cayuse war and became Indian superintendent from 1853 to 1857. Pursuing a career in state politics
he was elected Speaker in the state House of Representatives and
a state Senator in Oregon during the Civil War.

His book is considered by collectors to be one of the best of
the overland narratives.

84. McGlashan, Charles Fayette. *History of the Donner party, a tragedy*
of the Sierras. Truckee, Calif., Crowley and McGlashan [1879].

Even before the discovery of gold, various groups of North
American settlers were migrating to California. As in the case

of Texas, the immigration to California occurred while the territory was still under Mexican control. While early settlers had come by sea, overland parties began to arrive by 1841. Immigration societies and booster organizations began to flourish in the East. Although the unstable situation occasioned by the Bear Flag Revolt in 1845 and then the Mexican War in 1846 reduced this flow, it by no means discouraged the settlers altogether. It was in 1846 that one of the most famous overland trips occurred—the fateful journey of the Donner Party.

The party was organized largely in Illinois by George and Jacob Donner and left Independence, Missouri in the spring of 1846. Although it may have been comprised of as many as two hundred persons during the course of the journey, there were ninety members proper, about half of whom survived a snowbound winter in the Rockies. The swirl of charges and claims which ensued produced a variety of accounts, but nearly all of the contemporary records appear in C. F. McGlashan's *History of the Donner Party*.

85. Edwards, Frank S. *A campaign in New Mexico with Colonel Doniphan*...Philadelphia, Carey and Hart, 1847.

The Mexican War from 1846 to 1848 was the logical result of American expansionist policy. Yet, the collision of national interests was further assured by twenty years of Mexican political instability, a dozen years of filibustering and atrocities, and months of diplomatic failure. Of the three major campaigns of the war, only that of Stephen W. Kearny was concerned with territory which became part of the United States. His "Army of the West" was given the task of winning New Mexico and southern California. Leaving Ft. Leavenworth in June, 1846, Kearny arrived at Santa Fe in August. Here he divided his force, leading one segment on to California, leaving another to garrison New Mexico, and dispatching a third under Colonel A. W. Doniphan to strike south toward the Mexican states of Chihuahua and Coahuila.

Encountering forces of Mexicans many times larger, and cut off from their base of supply, Doniphan's Missouri Volunteers

BRONCO BUSTERS SADDLING.
(original size)
From March of America Series No. 99

traveled 3,200 miles by land and 2,000 miles by water in the course of twelve months. On their way into Mexico, where they joined forces with General Wool, they fought three engagements. The total command never numbered more than a thousand. One of the volunteers, Frank S. Edwards, quartermaster sergeant during the expedition, has left us the most readable account of the march.

86. Buffum, Edward Gould. *Six months in the gold mines...* Philadelphia, Lea and Blanchard, 1850.

Of all the events which influenced western migration, the news of gold in California in 1849 was probably second only to the news of Columbus's discovery itself. Towns blossomed in the desert overnight. Often like desert flowers they faded and were gone as quickly. But each new strike brought forth more gold seekers who came by steamer, stage, covered wagon, on horseback, on foot, and as far as they could by rail. What had been only a sparsely settled, sleepy Mexican territory became the pot of gold at the end of the American rainbow of westward expansion.

One of the earliest authentic accounts of California during the Gold Rush is E. Gould Buffum's *Six Months in the Gold Mines.* Buffum had been in California during the Mexican War as a member of the 7th Regiment, New York Volunteers. When gold was discovered at Sutter's Mill, he stayed in California and thus provided us with an eyewitness account of the dynamics of greed and economic growth.

87. Aldrich, Lorenzo D. *A journal of the overland route to California and the gold mines.* Lansingburgh, N. Y., Kirkpatrick, 1851.

Unlike today's vacation trip to California, in 1849 "getting there" was hardly "half the fun." Distance, disease, hostile Indians and natural calamities all took their toll of the Forty-niners. Yet the fact that more than half of the one hundred thousand residents of California at the end of 1849 had migrated there within six months is evidence enough of the great drawing power of the discovery of gold.

Lorenzo D. Aldrich of Lansingburgh, New York was one who found the lure of gold irresistible. While he left us little information about life and his experiences in the gold fields, the diary of his journey to California via Santa Fe, Tucson, and the Gila River is perhaps the first account of a trip across Arizona by a civilian. The other possible first account is the journal of James O. Pattie, published in 1831, the validity of which has long been in question. The road taken by Aldrich had been opened up during the Mexican War by the Mormon Battalion. It was later used, in part, for the southern, transcontinental railroad. Aldrich's diary was brought to an abrupt end by his death as he was making the return trip by way of the Isthmus of Panama. There are only a half dozen known copies of his work in existence.

88. Stansbury, Howard. *An expedition to the valley of the Great Salt Lake of Utah...* London, Low, 1852.

Using the Frémont reports about the Salt Lake and the Great Basin as a guide, the first party of Mormon immigrants set out across Iowa under the leadership of Brigham Young in the summer of 1847. Leaving behind them the persecution, from their earlier attempts at settlement in Ohio, Missouri, and Illinois, this vanguard of the "Saints" began what was to be one of the largest and best organized migrations to the far West. Two years later when Captain Howard Stansbury visited their settlement at Salt Lake, they had already made the desert bloom and had developed their patterns of community life.

Stansbury was an officer in the Army Topographical Engineers. He was assigned to make a comprehensive study of the Salt Lake region from the geological formations to the local religious customs. Government interest in the area stemmed from a concern to provide Oregon-bound immigrants more protection on the trail, and from a desire to find a possible alternative to the proposed southwestern route for a transcontinental railroad.

Stansbury's expedition provided needed information about potential supply roads to the Oregon Trail, a map of the Great

Salt Lake, one of the few unbiased views of Mormon life, and a new, more direct, eastern route to Salt Lake, which would in the future be utilized by the Overland Stage, the Pony Express, and the Union Pacific Railroad. In addition, his report—first issued as a Senate document and later published commercially—was full of a variety of scientific findings.

89. Delano, Alonzo. *Life on the plains and among the diggings*...Auburn, Miller, Orton & Mulligan, 1854.

In 1849, Alonzo Delano was urged by his physician to go west in hopes of improving his health. "About this time," he writes, "the astonishing accounts of the vast deposits of gold in California reached us, and besides the fever of the body, I was suddenly seized with the fever of the mind for gold...." He left for California to seek a cure for both mind and body. His trip west and wanderings throughout California in the period of the Gold Rush produced what has been noted as "one of the most interesting of all California books."

Delano became a prosperous banker in Grass Valley, California and was the author of a number of books and pamphlets on the state. His first work was published in 1854; it was reprinted several times, attesting to its influence. He found health, too, for he lived to a good age.

90. Manly, William Lewis. *Death Valley in '49*...San Jose, Calif., Pacific Tree and Vine, 1894.

One of the most obvious, yet nonetheless important, aspects of westward expansion was the relatively short time within which a huge population was transplanted across a continent. Nothing in the previous 350 years of westward migration quite compared with the mid-19th century movement. Such restlessness and mobility becomes even more impressive when related to the life of a particular individual.

William Lewis Manly was such an individual. Born to the woods and stony slopes of Vermont in 1820, at age ten he accompanied an uncle west to Ohio and Michigan in search of a family homestead. Ten years later, he and a companion were hunting game in Wisconsin, and in another decade, 1849, he was a member of a wagon train bound for California.

The trip to California comprises the greatest part of his account. To avoid the dangers of the late season in the high Sierras, his party went south from Salt Lake City, hoping to reach Los Angeles instead of proceeding west toward Sacramento. In doing so they became one of the first groups to cross Death Valley and the Mojave Desert, and nearly lost their lives doing so.

Although Manly wrote his impressions of this feat shortly thereafter, it remained in manuscript form and became mutilated. Some forty years later he again put down his reminiscences, which were published in 1894.

91. Colt, Mrs. Miriam (Davis). *Went to Kansas; being a thrilling account of an ill-fated expedition...*Watertown [N.Y.], Ingalls, 1862.

Not all those who started west in the mid-19th century found a land of plenty. Many became ill and lost their lives; others lost their fortunes and returned east. Miriam Colt's *Went to Kansas* is one of the few stories by a woman of life on the plains, its disappointments, its disasters. It is also the story of one of many utopian schemes and of the Kansas Territory in the turbulent days of the 1850's when it was torn between Northern and Southern factions.

In 1856 Mrs. Colt and her family went to the Kansas Territory under the auspices of the Vegetarian Company. This company and another, the Octagon Settlement Company, were formed to build a community at Neosho, Kansas. Both organizations were inspired by Henry S. Clubb of New York City, a temperance worker and reformer. The companies' plan of settlement called for tracts of land two miles square, to be cut up into sixteen triangular farms, forming an octagon, with a village in the center of each. The corner triangles were to be used as pasture and timber land.

Nothing was done by the trustees of the company to prepare community facilities for the settlers. Upon arriving, many of the settlers became disgusted and turned back. Others, like the Colt family, stayed on, hoping to translate the "dream community" into a reality. Without proper implements for conquering the prairie, and plagued by disease, they too, were finally forced to leave.

Mrs. Colt's book is in diary and letter form; her remarks are chatty, her descriptions sometimes melodramatic. Yet her story is one of tragedy: a glimpse of disillusionment, the dissolution of a "stillborn" utopia, and of the harsh realities of frontier prairie life.

92. Greeley, Horace. *An overland journey, from New York to San Francisco, in the summer of 1859.* New York, Saxton, Barker, 1860.

Horace Greeley was one of the few important, national exponents of western expansion who actually went west himself. In the summer of 1859, the founder and editor of the influential New York *Tribune* traveled by rail, horseback and stagecoach to California. In a series of letters sent back to his paper he commented about the perils of border life in "bleeding Kansas," the Gold Rush in Colorado, the Mormons in Utah, and finally California.

Greeley's book, *An Overland Journey*, published in 1860, was a "first" in many ways. He was the first major editor to make a trip to the Pacific coast. He was on the scene when the mining boom hit Colorado, and his two hour interview with Brigham Young was one of the earliest examples of this now familiar reportorial technique.

At the conclusion of his description he could not resist editorializing on the need and efficacy of building a railroad from Missouri to California. Authorities have credited his support with hastening the advent of such a railroad. The copy of the work used in the Series is from the General Library at the University of Michigan.

93. Whymper, Frederick. *Travel and adventure in the territory of Alaska...* London, Murray, 1868.

In the spring of 1867 with the purchase of Alaska from Russia, the continental dimensions of the "manifest destiny" of the

United States were realized. Almost no one knew anything about this vast territory; its purchase was derided as folly. It was believed to be a land of "icebergs, polar bears, volcanoes, and earthquakes." One of the earliest books offering accurate information about this new purchase was Frederick Whymper's *Travel and Adventure in the Territory of Alaska.*

Whymper, a young Englishman, was in the Pacific Northwest during the years from 1862 to 1867. Principally engaged by the Russo-American Telegraph Expedition, he was a member of the exploratory party to the Yukon Basin. The telegraph enterprise was an effort to link North America and Europe by an overland wire through Alaska and Siberia. The successful laying of an Atlantic cable in 1866 made this 6,000 mile venture unprofitable. Although the project was abandoned the observations and experiences of Whymper, as well as his drawings, were one worthwhile result.

94. Bowles, Samuel. *Across the continent: a summer's journey to the Rocky mountains, the Mormons, and the Pacific states...* Springfield, Mass., Bowles, 1865.

Samuel Bowles' *Across the Continent* was the first of three books which he wrote about the West. *The Switzerland of America* and *Our New West* appeared in 1869. Samuel Bowles was the editor of the Springfield, Massachusetts *Republican,* one of the most influential papers of the Northeast. Like Horace Greeley, Bowles was an ardent expansionist, a railroad booster, and a partisan Republican.

Across the Continent is the compiled dispatches Bowles sent to his newspaper while on a western trip by rail and stagecoach with Congressman Schuyler Colfax, Speaker of the House. In his account of the journey the political aspects of the junket are subordinate to the impressions of the Rocky Mountains, the Mormons, the Nevada mines, San Francisco, Chinese immigration, and the Oregon and Washington territories. The central theme of the work is the need for a transcontinental railroad.

Critical, concise, perceptive, and prejudiced, Bowles found much about the West which he disliked but more which confirmed his hopes and enthusiasm.

95. Dimsdale, Thomas Josiah. *The vigilantes of Montana, or Popular justice in the Rocky mountains*...Virginia City, M. T., Montana Post, 1866.

> *The Vigilantes of Montana* is one of the chief sources used by dramatists and novelists in their creation of the "western." The violent territorial times of the early 1860's in Montana were the days of miners, saloons, dance-hall girls and frontier justice. The book is a veritable catalogue of terms and phrases which have become clichés through repetition in movies and on television. It is the story of the crimes of the Plummer gang and how they were brought to justice.
>
> Thomas Dimsdale, the author, was a British-born editor of the *Montana Post Press* in Virginia City from 1863 to 1865. His account of the rise of the Vigilantes first appeared in the columns of his newspaper, but was offered in book form in 1866. Crude and unpolished as the society it described, this now rare work was the first book printed in Montana.

96. McCoy, Joseph Geiting. *Historic sketches of the cattle trade of the West and Southwest.* Kansas City, Mo., Ramsey, Millett & Hudson, 1874.

> Joseph G. McCoy's *Historic Sketches of the Cattle Trade* is a basic source for the history of the cattle kingdom. McCoy himself was largely responsible for transforming the cattle business into a great industry. Until 1866 cattle raising was limited largely to Texas and the high plains of Montana. During the Civil War the Texas herds increased rapidly but there was no way to bring them to market. McCoy, an Illinois meat buyer, established a depot at Abilene, Kansas on the line of the Kansas Pacific Railroad and urged the Texans to drive their herds north. Abilene was the first of many such "cow towns." McCoy was responsible for opening other markets at Wichita and Cottonwood Falls, and made the Chisholm Trail a major route to market.
>
> Within twenty years, 1867-1887, the growth of the western railroad network made cattle raising a very profitable pursuit

and succeeded in filling in the last major gap in the continental expansion of the United States, the grasslands of the Great Plains.

97. Dodge, Grenville Mellen. *How we built the Union Pacific railway, and other railway papers and addresses.* Washington, Govt. Print. Office, 1910. 1st Address only.

The coming of the railroad made full scale development of the West's natural resources possible and forever closed the debate about whether the westernmost settlements were beyond the area which the United States might reasonably be expected to secure. Railways supported and supplied the already existing mining industry, they brought the Great Plains cattle industry into being, and they enabled the final settlement of the West by farmers.

The clamor for a transcontinental road had begun just after the great gold rush of 1849. Not even the Civil War could distract or divert interest and energy from it. In 1862 Congress authorized two companies, the Central Pacific and the Union Pacific, to begin work. The Central Pacific was to begin at San Francisco and extend east, and the Union Pacific from Omaha west. Subsidized by grants of land which the railroad could sell and spurred on by promises of additional land for each mile of track laid, the competition between the two companies became one of the great races of history.

One of the men who played a prominent role in this race was Grenville M. Dodge of the Union Pacific Railroad. Recently, Dodge and his writings, notably *How We Built the Union Pacific Railway*, have been challenged on the grounds that Dodge distorted the part he played in the building of the road. It is argued that Dodge was not a key figure in selecting the route, surveying it, or supervising the construction as he seems to claim, but rather his role was that of diplomat and administrative organizer.

Even with such a revision in the traditional evaluation of Dodge's part, and even discounting his use of the first person in describing the building of the road, the merit of an account of such a feat by a participant still cannot be denied.

98. King, Charles. *Campaigning with Crook and stories of Army life.* New York, Harper, 1890.

Practically the last stage of the march of American civilization across the continent was the complete subjugation and disposition of the American Indian. As early as the 1850's when the mining frontier began to move from West to East and was joined in the 1860's by the twin developments of the railroad and the cattle industry, land which had been set aside as the permanent domain of the Indians was increasingly threatened with intrusion and appropriation. First the mountain tribes and then the plains tribes resisted these incursions. Between 1866 and 1891 there were a dozen major campaigns.

Of the major descriptions and insights to army life which resulted from this bloody concluding chapter, Charles King's *Campaigning With Crook* deserves a place of recognition both because it portrays one of the significant soldiers of the period, George Crook, and because it is an account of one of the key campaigns of the Indian War, the 1876 Sioux Uprising. Crook, though relentless and vigorous in prosecuting his orders, was likewise steadfast in his belief that the Indian must be accorded participation in American society.

Charles King, who was a soldier most of his life, was descended from Rufus King of New York, a signer of the Constitution. Born in Milwaukee in 1844 he learned to write and to soldier from his father, who edited the Milwaukee *Sentinel* and commanded the Iron Brigade in the Civil War. In his lifetime King wrote nearly sixty works, most of them fiction, many of them on army life. Three of these are included in the volume on Crook which was published in 1890. This edition was withdrawn by the publishers because King falsely accused a newspaper correspondent by the name of Davenport of cowardice (pp. 153-155). King made apologies in a subsequent edition of the same year. The work first appeared in the columns of the *Sentinel* and was published in paperback by the newspaper in 1880.

99. Roosevelt, Theodore. *Ranch life and the hunting-trail.* New York, Century, 1899.

Within the lifetime of Theodore Roosevelt, the United States made the transition from a predominantly rural, underdeveloped nation to an industrial world power, from a country with what seemed like inexhaustible natural resources to a land conscious of the need for conservation. In *Ranch Life and the Hunting Trail* Roosevelt, one of the first Americans to stress conservation, joined with Frederic Remington, one of the foremost artists of the West, to depict in text and tone the true nature of life on the northern plains. Remington contributed nearly a hundred illustrations to the work.

Roosevelt had come to the Dakota Badlands in 1883 primarily to hunt, but soon engaged in cattle ranching. His descriptions of ranch life and the vignettes of cowboy types are drawn from this experience. His firsthand knowledge and appreciation of the transient or ephemeral qualities of western resources as well as his love of the outdoors caused him to champion conservation.

100. Turner, Frederick Jackson. "The significance of the frontier in American history," in *Annual report of the American Historical Association for the year 1893.* Washington, Govt. Print. Office, 1894.

The famous essay by historian Frederick Jackson Turner on "The Significance of the Frontier in American History," read at a world congress of historians in Chicago in 1893, was both the epitaph of an era and a new departure in American self-criticism. Turner began by noting that as of 1890 there was no longer anything which could be described as a line of frontier, and then proposed an evaluation of the influence this frontier had exerted on American society and personality. His frontier thesis became a landmark in American historiography. Though somewhat reworked and refined in the last seventy years it remains a major interpretation of the American experience. For the March of America Series it forms a fitting conclusion to four hundred years of narrative and eyewitness accounts by men and women who participated in the westward expansion of American civilization.

Research Sources

Just as each participant in the four centuries-long reconnaissance of North America necessarily relied on the cumulative knowledge of successive predecessors, so the compiler of a series like the *March of America* is inevitably obliged to the many scholars in the field who have preceded him and assembled the bibliographical data. The idea of bringing together and reprinting American exploration accounts and travel narratives is not itself original with this Series. Certainly J. Franklin Jameson's *Original Narratives of Early American History*, 19 vols. (New York, 1906-1917 and 1952) is a classic collection for the colonial field. To a lesser extent, J. B. McMaster's *The Trail Makers*, 17 vols. (New York, 1903-1905) which also appeared under the series title *American Explorers*, 17 vols. (New York, 1922) deserves mention. For the late 18th and early 19th centuries we have had R. G. Thwaites' *Early Western Travels, 1748-1846*, 32 vols. (Cleveland, 1904-1907) and *The Lakeside Classics*, vols. 14-55 (Chicago, 1916-1957) under the editorship of Milo Quaife. The strength of this new Series lies in encompassing, for the first time, the entire period of discovery and expansion—1493 to 1893—and, by means of photoduplication processes, offering the truest facsimiles yet produced. In addition the Series offers important rare titles that have never before been reprinted while making available again works which have been previously offered in limited editions or are now out of print. The debt incurred in the selection of these works is owed to a wide variety of sources.

Aside from the introductory notes in the various series previously cited, there were a number of general works which proved basic. Both the *Harvard Guide to American History* (Cambridge, Mass., 1960) and the Library of Congress' *A Guide to the Study of the United States of America* (Washington, D.C., 1960) contain special sections on travel and description. Two other bibliographies bear mention as general surveys: J. N. Larned, *The Literature of American History* (Columbus, Ohio, 1953) and Thomas D. Clark, *Travels in the Old South*, 3 vols. (Norman, Okla., 1956-1959). Both of these works go beyond the typical imprint bibliographical lists by providing detailed annotations on the content as well as offering some critical evaluation. This is particularly true of Clark's work which is additionally useful because his definition of the "South" is so broadly conceived as to include works on the entire Ohio and Mississippi valleys. The best single text for the study of the exploration and settlement of North America is Ray A. Billington's *Westward Expansion* (New York, 1960). Although some of the generalizations do not bear up under scrutiny, nothing else in the field comes close to filling the large canvas of the moving frontier so well. Equal in scope to the text is the nearly one hundred pages of annotated bibliography which is the most comprehensive compilation available on the recent books and journal articles. For pinpointing elusive data Richard B. Morris' *Encyclopedia of American History* (New York, 1961) and the *Dictionary of American Biography*, 22 vols. (New York, 1928-1944) are extremely handy.

In researching the works of the period before 1800, there are, of course, the basic bibliographies of Americana: Joseph Sabin, *A Dictionary of Books Relating to America*, 29 vols. (New York, 1868-1936), Charles Evans, *American Bibliography*, 14 vols. (Chicago and Worcester, Mass., 1903-1959), and Elihu Dwight Church, *Catalogue of Books Relating to the Discovery and Early History of North and South America*, 5 vols. (New York, 1907). Henry Harrisse, *Bibliotheca Americana Vetutissima* (New York, 1866) is good in unraveling some of the informational snarl associated with the earliest accounts and their compilers. Boies Penrose, *Travels and Discovery in the Renaissance, 1420-1626* (Cambridge, Mass., 1952), a more modern work in many ways, has a very inclusive essay on early geographical literature in Chapter 17, clearly, concisely, and informatively written. R. W. G. Vail's *The Voice of the Old Frontier* (Philadelphia, 1949) was particularly helpful in focusing on the frontiersmen's own stories, the Indian captivities, and the promotional tracts.

Three works, however, were of invaluable assistance: Justin Winsor's *Narrative and Critical History of America*, 8 vols. (Boston, 1884-1889), William L. Clements, *The William L. Clements Library of Americana at the University of Michigan* (Ann Arbor, 1923), and John Bartlett Brebner's *The Explorers of North America* (Garden City, N. Y., 1955). Winsor's work, though eighty years old, has yet to be matched for its combination of historical narrative and literary criticism. At the end of each chapter there is a critical essay on sources. Similarly Mr. Clements' discussion of rare Americana presents bibliogaphical data while noting the significance of the works based on their historical content and influence. Brebner's book, though more a formal history of exploration from Columbus to Lewis and Clark, has excellent suggestions on sources and contains a crisp, yet detailed exposition. Another extremely well-written work on American exploration to the time of Lewis and Clark is Bernard DeVoto's *The Course of Empire* (Boston, 1962); it is less helpful for bibliographical questions, however.

A number of other works were useful for more limited topics within the period before 1800 such as Clarence W. Alvord and Lee Bidgood's *The First Explorations of the Trans-Allegheny Region by Virginians, 1650-1674* (Cleveland, 1912), James C. McCoy's *Jesuit Relations of Canada* (Paris,

1937), Howard H. Peckham's *Captured by Indians* (New Brunswick, N. J., 1954), and Sir Maurice Holmes' *Captain Cook, R.N., F.R.S. A Bibliographical Excursion* (London, 1952). Several state bibliographies were also helpful, their bibliographical chauvinism embracing the literature of an entire region. Such works as Elizabeth Baer's *Seventeenth Century Maryland, A Bibliography* (Baltimore, 1949), which is very good, encompasses the important titles of most of the middle colonies plus Virginia; and Albert Harry Greenly's *A Selective Bibliography of Important Books, Pamphlets and Broadsides Relating to Michigan History* (Lunenburg, Vt., 1958) covers the exploratory period in eastern Canada and most of the Great Lakes. Solon J. Buck's *Travel and Description, 1765-1865* (Springfield, 1914), a part of the *Collections* of the Illinois State Historical Library series, is good for the Mid-west in general. Other useful state or regional books were Robert E. and Robert G. Cowan's *A Bibliography of the History of California, 1510-1930,* 2 vols. (San Francisco, 1933), Charles R. Hildeburn, *The Issues of the Press in Pennsylvania, 1685-1784,* 2 vols. (Philadelphia, 1885), Clarence C. Hulley's *Alaska: 1741-1953* (Portland, Ore., 1953), and Henry R. Wagner, *The Spanish Southwest, 1542-1794,* (Berkeley, 1924).

The period from 1800 down to the close of the frontier is not as well endowed with formal bibliographies as the previous eras. This is particularly true for the years following the Civil War. For the first half of the 19th century there is, of course, Henry R. Wagner and Charles L. Camp's *The Plains and Rockies* (Columbus, Ohio, 1953). Aside from being the only major work for the period and somewhat selective, it is also very good. Usually some brief description of the contents appears along with references to related works or authorities. Other aids in this period, but even more limited than Wagner-Camp, are Robert R. Hubach's *Early Midwestern Travel Narratives, 1634-1850* (Detroit, 1961), Ralph Leslie Rusk, *The Literature of the Middle Western Frontier,* 2 vols. (New York, 1926), Peter G. Thompson, *A Bibliography of the State of Ohio* (Cincinnati, 1880), R. E. Banta, *Indiana Authors and Their Books, 1816-1916* (Crawfordsville, Ind., 1949), J. Christian Bay, *Three Handfuls of Western Books* (Cedar Rapids, Ia., 1941), and Thomas W. Streeter, *Bibliography of Texas, 1795-1845,* Part III—United States and European Imprints Relating to Texas, 2 vols. (Cambridge, Mass., 1960).

Several histories served as supplements to the bibliographies or in place of them in the later part of the 19th century research. Among the most useful were Ray A. Billington's *The Far Western Frontier* (New York, 1956), Bayrd Still, *The West* (New York, 1961), E. W. Gilbert, *The Exploration of Western America* (London, 1933), William H. Goetzmann, *Army Exploration in the American West* (New Haven, 1959), Walter Prescott Webb, *The Great Plains* (Boston, 1931), Carl I. Wheat, *Mapping the Transmississippi West, 1540-1861,* 5 vols. (San Francisco, 1959), and Ernest S. Osgood, *The Day of the Cattleman* (Minneapolis, 1929).